# Maker Innovations Series

I0016807

Jump start your path to discovery with the Apress Maker Innovations series! From the basics of electricity and components through to the most advanced options in robotics and Machine Learning, you'll forge a path to building ingenious hardware and controlling it with cutting-edge software. All while gaining new skills and experience with common toolsets you can take to new projects or even into a whole new career.

The Apress Maker Innovations series offers projects-based learning, while keeping theory and best processes front and center. So you get hands-on experience while also learning the terms of the trade and how entrepreneurs, inventors, and engineers think through creating and executing hardware projects. You can learn to design circuits, program AI, create IoT systems for your home or even city, and so much more!

Whether you're a beginning hobbyist or a seasoned entrepreneur working out of your basement or garage, you'll scale up your skillset to become a hardware design and engineering pro. And often using low-cost and open-source software such as the Raspberry Pi, Arduino, PIC microcontroller, and Robot Operating System (ROS). Programmers and software engineers have great opportunities to learn, too, as many projects and control environments are based in popular languages and operating systems, such as Python and Linux.

If you want to build a robot, set up a smart home, tackle assembling a weather-ready meteorology system, or create a brand-new circuit using breadboards and circuit design software, this series has all that and more! Written by creative and seasoned Makers, every book in the series tackles both tested and leading-edge approaches and technologies for bringing your visions and projects to life.

More information about this series at https://link.springer.com/bookseries/17311.

# The Ultimate LEGO Technic Book

## How to Build Complex Vehicles and Machines

Mark Rollins

Apress®

*The Ultimate LEGO Technic Book: How to Build Complex Vehicles and Machines*

Mark Rollins
Pullman, WA, USA

ISBN-13 (pbk): 979-8-8688-0792-3          ISBN-13 (electronic): 979-8-8688-0793-0
https://doi.org/10.1007/979-8-8688-0793-0

## Copyright © 2024 by Mark Rollins

Managing Director, Apress Media LLC: Welmoed Spahr
Acquisitions Editor: Miriam Haidara
Development Editor: James Markham
Coordinating Editor: Jessica Vakili

Cover designed by eStudioCalamar

Distributed to the book trade worldwide by Apress Media, LLC, 1 New York Plaza, New York, NY 10004, U.S.A. Phone 1-800-SPRINGER, fax (201) 348-4505, e-mail orders-ny@springer-sbm.com, or visit www.springeronline.com. Apress Media, LLC is a California LLC and the sole member (owner) is Springer Science + Business Media Finance Inc (SSBM Finance Inc). SSBM Finance Inc is a **Delaware** corporation.

For information on translations, please e-mail booktranslations@springernature.com; for reprint, paperback, or audio rights, please e-mail bookpermissions@springernature.com.

Apress titles may be purchased in bulk for academic, corporate, or promotional use. eBook versions and licenses are also available for most titles. For more information, reference our Print and eBook Bulk Sales web page at http://www.apress.com/bulk-sales.

Any source code or other supplementary material referenced by the author in this book is available to readers on GitHub (https://github.com/Apress). For more detailed information, please visit https://www.apress.com/gp/services/source-code.

If disposing of this product, please recycle the paper

# Table of Contents

# About the Author

 **Mark Rollins** has been an established writer for two decades, delving into tech and gadget blogging 20 years ago, contributing to various consumer electronics-related websites. Over the last 15 years, he has successfully managed TheGeekChurch.com, boasting a tech website, a YouTube channel (500+ subscribers), and a TikTok channel (20,000+ followers). Mark recently collaborated with Pullman Marketing, showcasing his skills. As a seasoned author, Mark has published six books with Apress, covering Android Marketing, LEGO, Kindle Fire, and UBTECH/Jimu Robots, displaying a diverse and comprehensive writing portfolio.

# About the Technical Reviewer

**Farzin Asadi** received his B.Sc. in Electronics Engineering, his M.Sc. in Control Engineering, and his Ph.D. in Mechatronics Engineering. Currently, he is with the Department of Computer Engineering at the Ostim Technical University, Ankara, Turkey. Dr. Asadi has published over 40 international papers and 29 books. His research interests include switching converters, control theory, robust control of power electronics converters, and robotics.

# CHAPTER 1

# Introduction

When LEGO was first released, it was looked at as a better type of building blocks. Just another way to make structures, and you could make something to the extent of complex dollhouses. It wasn't until the Expert sets when LEGO realized the potential of their building bricks to create complex machines, but to achieve this, LEGO had to change from the brick up, creating a new type of building block for its new creations.

It wasn't just that the models were larger, but it was about what they could do. Not only could you create a car with some interesting bodywork, but you could also steer that car. You could even create construction machines like bulldozers and forklifts that had some very realistic properties of operation.

These "Expert sets," later rebranded as Technic, truly opened up the world of LEGO builders, and it has been going strong for over 35 years. The pieces have been continuously evolving, and the challenge keeps getting greater for experienced builders of LEGO.

If you're reading this book, then it means that you wish to take your LEGO Technic to the next level, even if you aren't certain what that is. When I wrote my first book about LEGO Technic, I was amazed to see how much I could do with these beams, levers, axles, and gears and the other basic and advanced LEGO hardware. I have written two books about LEGO Technic, and I really wanted to highlight what I have learned since then.

© Mark Rollins 2024
M. Rollins, *The Ultimate LEGO Technic Book*, Maker Innovations Series,
https://doi.org/10.1007/979-8-8688-0793-0_1

We will discuss the basics of LEGO Technic pieces later in this chapter; for now, I think it would be appropriate to discuss the history of LEGO Technic and what it has become since its initial release back in the late 1970s.

# History of LEGO Technic

When it comes to who founded LEGO, it gets attributed to Ole Kirk Kristiansen in 1932, who actually made toys out of wood in his home country of Denmark. This family-owned business has since been passed down from father to son.

You will notice that LEGO is often used in all capitals, but it is not an acronym. It stems from two Danish words meaning "play well," and it also means "I put together" in Latin. The LEGO name was officially used in 1936, but only on their highly crafted wooden toys, and it wasn't until 10 years later when the Kristiansen family invests in plastic.

In about 1949, the LEGO bricks begin to look like what they are now...somewhat. Think of the basic 2 × 4 brick, but empty on the bottom, and you have it. It was called the Automatic Binding Brick, and the original catalog from that year has some of the early sets, which were small houses that looked very blocky, sort of like Minecraft. These houses had roofs that did not slope, but there were already window-like pieces that appeared to show off what type of detail these early LEGO construction sets were capable of.

By 1953, the LEGO name appears on every brick, just like it appears on every stud (the round section of the brick), with construction kits of LEGO Mursten (LEGO bricks) to encourage creative play. LEGO drops the name of Automatic Binding Bricks and begins to produce brochures that showed models that could be produced from extra sets. In 1955, there is a town plan that has bricks of all kinds of interesting shapes, even with curves. There are vehicles on these catalogs, but it doesn't look like the user could assemble these, like the buildings.

It wasn't until 1958 that the coupling principle is patented, which really highlights the "clicking together" that LEGO is truly known for. It was very apparent that the family realized its potential and encouraged building up of LEGO bricks in order to stimulate children's creativity.

Then in 1960, a fire destroys the company's wooden toy warehouse, which marks the time when LEGO begins to stop production of their wooden toys. The LEGO toys begin to flourish, with wheeled creations in 1962, and by 1965, new catalogs begin to come out each year that highlight the growth of the company.

If you look into these catalogs, you are going to see how Technic slowly starts to be conceived. Even as early as 1966, LEGO begins to market motorized bricks, which comes in really handy for making trains, which LEGO marketed very early with complex track systems. It is important to note the trains were much larger in scale than the buildings in the town playsets released at around the same time. By 1968, the vehicles started to become very detailed with hinge pieces and even cranes, but they were not very mechanical, but the scale that is visible in Technic is there.

***Figure 1-1.*** *Early LEGO motors and trains, a definite grandfather of LEGO Technic*

In 1970, LEGO sets began to be smaller, as the buildings and cars were designed to be embraced by people who were 4–5 bricks tall. There was a set around this time (set number 140) called the Bricks and Motor set that was a set in the right direction to making creator-made vehicles that could run on battery-powered motors. Then, in 1971, LEGO gear pieces came in, creating the possibility of LEGO motion. These gears don't look like anything they would make today, but it was a start. Around this time, LEGO started to put out sets with axles, and this particular part has changed very little since its initial introduction.

In the 1974 catalog, there is a page that just says "Get Things Moving," and these are the first indicators of Technic. There is even a crane that has pieces with the holes on the sides, which were indicative of the first LEGO Technic bricks.

***Figure 1-2.*** *From the 1976 catalog, this shows LEGO vehicles in a bigger scale*

Two years later, a catalog appears that is marked the LEGO Experts guide to 1976. This has a motorized kit that is a bit more advanced, and there are also some pretty advanced looking models in the regular catalog, and one of them, a Formula 1 racer, looks like a go-cart.

These were Hobby sets, and they got really detailed with cars like 1913 Cadillac, 1909 Rolls-Royce, and 1926 Renault and other projects like a Thatcher Perkins Locomotive.

It was in the late 1970s that Kjeld Kirk Kristiansen develops a "system with the system" to offer children the right products at the right age and the right purpose. This allowed the company to really look at children of all ages and create products for certain age groups.

From here, it was when the company began to branch in two separate directions as far as creating products for the audience of children that had outgrown Duplo. LEGO was really growing in popularity and profits, and the late 1970s were a time to create systems that still remain a part of the company, such as the Space systems, the Knight/Castle systems, and the Town system, which was later rebranded as City.

**Figure 1-3.**  *One of the first appearances of LEGO Expert sets in the late 1970s, with all new versions of LEGO pieces*

This huge shift in LEGO is where the LEGO Expert Builder sets came about. This is when the company took full advantage of the LEGO bricks with holes in the sides, and it could create vehicles that were far more advanced. These were not just toys, but modeling kits that could really show older builders just how motors and steering actually worked.

Personally, I remember being fascinated by the go-cart (set 948, see Figure 1-3) with its rack-and-pinion steering function. There were other sets that had features like a forklift that could elevate its prongs, not to mention a crane with more advanced functions of any LEGO crane ever before. There was even a kit that you could purchase that would allow the user to motorize these creations.

Like all LEGO sets, new models were produced every year, and eventually, the name of Expert Builder got changed to Technic. Not only did it produce sets that specialized in a certain type of vehicle model, but there were a lot of great Universal Building sets that you could buy during that time in the late 1970s and early 1980s.

By 1985, the company was adding air pressure as their coolest feature. It's something that isn't really in modern sets. By 1988, Technic went new directions as it created creations that could transform. They also attempted these giant figurines that were made for the scale of the vehicles. These larger figures have since been discontinued.

***Figure 1-4.*** *Advancements of LEGO Technic in the 1980s*

In 1989, LEGO brought back the Universal Building sets, as well as some models like large Auto Chassis (8865) and Prop Plane (8855). On a somewhat related note, LEGO was also attempting a new type of structure with the model team, which were a lot bigger models with more detail.

The year of 1990 is when Technic saw this programmable control center, which had two 9V motors for some very advanced motorized models like a robot, a crane, and a drawing machine. This type of functionality was the first attempt of making something that was essentially programmable in the LEGO world, with greater advancements in that technology advancing later.

In the early 1990s, new types of LEGO pieces came to the Technic set. These were pieces that didn't have studs on them. It was slowly evolving, and the Night Chopper (set 8825) There were pieces on this set that were flat and with holes, but somewhat different than the LEGO Technic pieces that had gone before it. Set 8207, the Dune Duster, is almost completely bereft of traditional LEGO brick.

There were all kinds of variations within Technic itself, which is characteristic of a lot of LEGO systems. For example, 1997 was the year of Bungee Blasters, as you pull them back and off they go. Technic had a set 8250 that was a sub with pneumatic, and it had these two interesting pieces with no studs on them. There was also a slight push for fiber optic lighting. Then, in 1998, LEGO introduced this series called Cyber Slam. Think of it as Rock 'em Sock 'em robots with these figures, because that Technic was still doing its "maxi-figs."

Also in 1998, something big yet little had happened. The old bricks were hardly being used. The traditional Technic bricks, which were essentially traditional LEGO bricks with holes in the sides, were replaced with beams, which had the holes, but not the studs.

In 1999, LEGO gave its Technic users throwbots, made under the Technic brand, that could throw discs. Newer models were under the "Tech Build" category.

In 2000, even *Star Wars* got into this. All models had virtually none of the old bricks, and there was some interesting detail work as far as these droids were concerned. For example, the Battle Droid (set 8001) was able to fold up and then rise to its feet at the touch of a button thanks to the help of some rubber bands and really nifty building techniques.

***Figure 1-5.*** *Various LEGO Technic sets inspired by Star Wars*

So yes, Technic was slightly veering away from its vehicle sets to focus more on robotics. There were sets like Slizer and Robot Riders. Not to mention Speed Slammers.

It was also in 2000 that the unveiling of MINDSTORMS occurred. This was an intelligent brick playset. All of the models were built with the new versions of the bricks and could be programmed. There was even a *Star Wars* version of it. MINDSTORMS had a second version with the NXT and then had a third version known as the EV3 on 2013. The MINDSTORMS system has been recently discontinued and had its last Robot Inventor product in 2020. I won't be focusing much on MINDSTORMS in this particular book, but I have written a book on the EV3 if you are interested.

***Figure 1-6.*** *LEGO MINDSTORMS series, with the first version, followed by NXT 2.0 and EV3*

In 2001, they revealed the Bionicle system, which was still under the Technic umbrella. These had various iterations in its decade-long run and even had a few direct-to-DVD movies. Technic pieces are used for the Bionicle series, but I won't be discussing any of the arms, legs, feet, or faces from that, as this series has also been discontinued.

Of course, Technic kept going with new models that just kept getting more and more advanced. In 2007, there was special edition known as Power Functions (not related to MINDSTORMS) where the motors could be remotely controlled. Of course, in an age where "there is an app for that," there is also an app for that known as LEGO Technic Control + as made for propelling a vehicle backwards and forwards and can even steer a vehicle as well.

LEGO Technic continues to thrive today, as the sports cars/race cars are always popular, along with motorcycles, not to mention airplanes and helicopters. There are even smaller scale kits, as well as big construction equipment like cranes, and small construction equipment available.

*Figure 1-7.* *Various LEGO kits throughout the years*

# Difference Between Technic and Regular LEGO

I hope you had a lot of fun with that trip down LEGO Technic memory lane, as I know I have. I wanted to talk about why I consider LEGO Technic and regular LEGO as separate entities, but still all part of the same LEGO family.

## Complexity

I think about Technic being different from traditional LEGO as a Duplo is different from LEGO. A kid of a certain age wouldn't be caught dead playing with Duplo because they are viewed as baby's toy. Not that a Duplo block won't fit with a traditional LEGO block, as they are made to be a regular traditional LEGO brick with an exact double proportion. Most traditional LEGO is based on stacking bricks in what is hopefully the strongest manner possible to make something aesthetically pleasing.

And of course, building with Technic is also something that is aesthetically pleasing, but the principles to building strong are different. I will have to admit that vehicles and machines have their set of aesthetics that make them attractive in their own way. However, Technic is all about having your end model do something, even if you don't "play" with it. The point is realism, and you want it to be able to steer because your actual, real life-sized car can steer.

In order to do that, you will need to use axles, gears, and all kinds of parts that could be confusing if you don't understand simple machines, and most younger kids do not. Some adults can't really identify LEGO Technic as LEGO, honestly.

## Scale

Most LEGO sets are designed with the same sort of scale. Once the minifig caught on, it set a size standard for LEGO. The fact that a minifig foot is about the size of a LEGO stud means that one foot equals one LEGO stud.

That is, if you were to create a house, car, castle, or spaceship, then you had better make certain that a minifig can fit in there, even if it is uncomfortable with the amount of space it has.

With Technic, the scale is much larger, and you would not want a minifig to try and drive a Technic vehicle. As I said before, LEGO used to make figures designed for Technic vehicles, but that has gone the way of dial-up Internet.

Part of building in Technic is about attention to detail, which can't be done on a minifig scale. Since the Technic vehicles are much larger in scale, details can be explored, which opens up the possibilities to what a Technic model can do.

# Can LEGO Technic and Traditional LEGO work together?

The short answer would be yes, and there are several traditional LEGO sets that include some pieces that I consider Technic pieces. There are also LEGO Technic sets that have many traditional LEGO pieces included.

For example, some traditional LEGO sets that have wheels often use an axle and a wheel in their construction. There are also LEGO Technic sets that include a lot of traditional bricks with an emphasis on tiles (flat or plate pieces with no studs on top) to add realism to vehicle creations.

The thing about using traditional LEGO with LEGO Technic, and vice versa, is that the two styles of bricks often stick out in the creation. I think the best way to compare traditional LEGO and LEGO Technic is to use an analogy, comparing 2D animation with 3D animation. Animation started with 2D to make cartoons that eventually looked good with the help of great artists hand drawing every single frame. Then when 3D came around, artists were also needed to make works that were almost photo-realistic in nature, and there was less work on a frame-by-frame level as the computer did the motion rendering.

I bring this up to emphasize that 2D animation is still used, and 3D is not "better" than it. You can use whatever style to make a story that work. Again, I'm not trying to say that one is better than the other, and I'm not saying that LEGO Technic is better than traditional LEGO. The problem is when you start mixing these together.

Sometimes, it comes across well, as the 1986 film *The Great Mouse Detective* had massive clock gears that were rendered in CG. It was in the Disney Renaissance where the CG backgrounds began to look like they dwarfed the characters, like the ballroom scene from *Beauty and the Beast* and the cave scene in *Aladdin*. One of the worst examples is Twentieth-Century Fox's animated *Titan A.E.*, where the spaceships looked very pristine and incredibly shiny and metallic with these 2D characters.

However, there are examples where mixing 2D and 3D work so well, that I had to be told that a 3D element was added. If you ever watched *The Iron Giant*, it is a great 2D animated film with a 3D addition of the giant in it. The same applies to *Treasure Planet*, with silver's artificial arm. In both cases, the 3D kind creates an otherworldly charm, which would stand out no matter how you rendered it.

For me, I see regular LEGO as 2D animation, and I see LEGO Technic as 3D animation. If you watch enough animation, then you know that 2D and 3D often don't look good together. Granted, it is easy to make 3D environments and put in hand-drawn animation, but it might not mix well.

For the most part, Technic has steered away from traditional bricks, even the Technic bricks that it used to have. I recently constructed a spaceship using LEGO Technic beams as a frame and then put LEGO plates (flat traditional LEGO pieces) as the body of this, and it worked quite well.

You may find that it is possible to build with both, and I discuss many different building techniques in this book.

# Places to Find LEGO Technic at a Low Price

Just to let you know, this book isn't the only one about LEGO that I intend to publish at this time, as I am also publishing a book about how to work with traditional LEGO as well.

In the other book about LEGO Worldbuilding and Architecture, I discussed where to obtain LEGO, focusing on eBay auctions to garage sales. I will have to say that the least expensive way to obtain LEGO is to get them from people giving them away, because nothing is cheaper than free.

I've had several people give them away and obtained some for myself. Most parents have kids that grow up with them, and then they kind of abandon them. They store them away, and the collection just sits in storage like the Our-Mom-a-Geddon from *Lego Movie 2*. Usually thrown away are the boxes and possibly the instructions, so all that is left is a disorganized mass that gets put in some kind of storage.

If you are wanting to do that, you might find someone willing to give away leftover LEGO Technic, but that can be difficult. Technic is so different; many users keep it separate, so you could luck out. However, a lot of parents don't care about separating the LEGO Technic from the traditional LEGO, so these specialized pieces literally get lost in the shuffle.

For me, I had obtained many Technic sets throughout the years and would often purchase newer sets if I thought they could help me build bigger and more complex models. Yes, that will cost you. Speaking of costing me, there was a time where I found really an untrustworthy website selling cheap sets and bought a whole bunch. I remember waiting quite a while for the order, and when it came, it was a sham. I'd rather not talk about that, no matter how interested you might be in hearing that story.

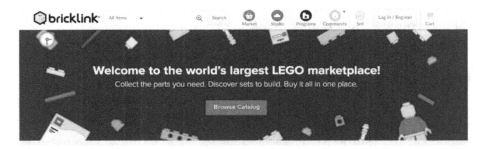

***Figure 1-8.*** *The BrickLink homepage, a good place to purchase individual LEGO Technic pieces*

Let the buyer beware, and chances are you need to be looking for specific pieces that come with most Technic sets. Therefore, I recommend going to places like BrickLink and others in order to obtain what pieces that you will need. I talk more about other places to find bricks in my book, so I'm going to proceed like you have many.

# Sorting Your LEGO Technic Pieces

When it comes to traditional LEGO, the pieces are so diverse, and I have a different method of doing that. Of course, I discuss that in my other book and the other video based on that chapter, but honestly, organizing LEGO Technic is a lot simpler as you can separate them into categories based on usage.

Since I work with a lot of LEGO Technic, it became necessary to just organize the pieces. After all, the point of this is to learn to plan as you build, and the last thing you want to do is sift through thousands of pieces just to find the one you need at one specific spot in your building.

As a kid, that works, I guess, but you really lose a lot of time sifting when you could be building. The best thing that you can do is separating different types of pieces in small drawers, like those found on tackleboxes. I purchased these at a retail store about a decade ago, and I devote certain sections to certain types of pieces. If you look at LEGO enthusiasts, they often have garages with drawers to house all their numerous pieces. So if they need a piece of a certain design with a specific color, bam, there it is.

When I talked about organizing pieces in my last video, I discussed phases. The first phase is organizing by size, then color, and then usage, and then actual piece. In case you don't know, every piece that LEGO creates has a specific designated number.

Personally, I don't have too many pieces of Technic, so I don't really consider color. I organize pretty much by shape, and the space that I put them in is so small; I can usually find the color that I need when I need it. I tend not to care too much about color when I build, because I'm not really going for aesthetics, but functionality. Not only that, some pieces only come in one color anyway.

# Bricks

When Technic, or Expert sets, as they were called back then, were unveiled, they created a new type of brick that was still discernible from the old one. The idea was pretty simple, as instead of attaching one brick to the top with the studs, one could go to the sides. Of course, if they were studded on both sides, then they would not so easily fit together, but with certain other pieces, such as the connector pegs (which we'll discuss later), you could fit them together.

I must admit that these Technic bricks, which were the basic units of building in the old Technic kits, have phased out these bricks for the beams, which I will discuss right now. I did want to bring them up because they can be used, but there won't be much to talk about here. In fact, I actually incorporate Technic bricks in my other book about LEGO Worldbuilding, which should be available at the time you are reading this book.

You might note how the studs are hollowed out on top, but not certain why that is.

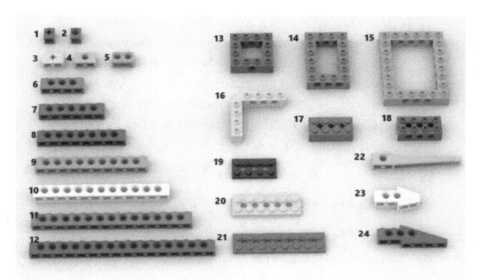

**Figure 1-9.** *Samples of LEGO Technic bricks*

1) Technic brick 1 × 1 with axle hole (73230): A typical 1 × 1 brick with an axle hole in the middle

2) Technic brick 1 × 1 with hole (6541): Another typical 1 × 1 brick with a Technic addition of a through hole. Generally, the number of through holes is equal to the number of studs, minus one, but this is one exception

3) Technic brick 1 × 2 with axle hole (32064): A 1 × 2 brick with an axle hole

4) Technic brick 1 × 2 with hole (3700): Typical round hole in a 1 × 2 typical brick

5) Technic brick 1 × 2 with holes (32000): Another exception to the number of through holes equal to the number of studs, minus one

6) Technic brick 1 × 4 with holes (3701): With one exception, LEGO Technic bricks generally have an even number of studs, and this is one of the smallest at a length of 4M with three round holes on the side. The rest of the Technic bricks increase by 2M or two studs, and the rule of the number of round holes on the side is equal to the number of studs, minus one

7) Technic brick 1 × 6 with holes (3894)

8) Technic brick 1 × 8 with holes (3702)

9) Technic brick 1 × 10 with holes (2730)

10) Technic brick 1 × 12 with holes (3895)

11) Technic brick 1 × 14 with holes (32018)

12) Technic brick 1 × 16 with holes (3703)

13) Technic brick 4 × 4 open center (32324): Of course, it is possible to create this piece with several other Technic brick pieces, but it is good to start a creation with a solid form such as this

14) Technic brick 4 × 6 open center (32531)

15) Technic brick 6 × 8 open center (32532)

16) Technic brick 5 × 5 right angle (32555): Like traditional LEGO bricks, LEGO Technic bricks come with corner pieces

17) Technic brick 2 × 4 with three axle holes (39789): This is a typical 2 × 4 brick with three axle holes in the middle

18) Technic brick 2 × 4 with holes on all sides (3709a):
A typical 2 × 4 brick with through holes on the
sides and top

19) Technic plate 2 × 4 with three holes (3709b): Like the
brick, the LEGO plate also had through holes, equal
to the number of pieces in the length, minus one

20) Technic plate 2 × 6 with five holes (32001)

21) Technic plate 2 × 8 with seven holes (3738)

22) Technic forklift fork (2823): This is essentially a 1 × 2
Technic brick with an odd extension that takes it to a
length of 6M. I believe it is called a fork as it used to
be used in LEGO sets with forklifts

23) Technic slope 4 × 1 × 2 1/3 (2743): LEGO Technic
used to have sets with airplanes that had these types
of LEGO bricks, before moving to beams

24) Technic slope 6 × 1 × 1 2/3 (2744)

# Beams

While Y2K didn't cause all the problems that we thought it might, 2000
was quite a year as Technic bricks were essentially phased out, with these
beams taking their place. These are now the basic units of building in
Technic, and there are no studs on top, or the bottom. All there are these
through holes.

It should be noted that until the bricks, which are usually even-
numbered studs (with the three being still very common), the beams are
usually odd-numbered. The exception being the two, which comes in this
one with an axle hole in one and a through hole in another, or just two
through holes. The longest beam is currently at 15.

In addition to the straight ones, there are two that come at right angles. This particular 2 × 4 has an axle hole, while the 3 × 5 has all through holes.

Then there are some beams which have this angle of 53.1 degrees on them. You might think it is a 45-degree angle, as that would be half of a right triangle, but these particular ones are at this angle for a reason. This reason is so you can make a triangular shape with this angle, but you will find the Pythagorean theorem doesn't really apply in a traditional sense.

Then there is this double angle beam, and this has two 45-degree angles to make this 90.

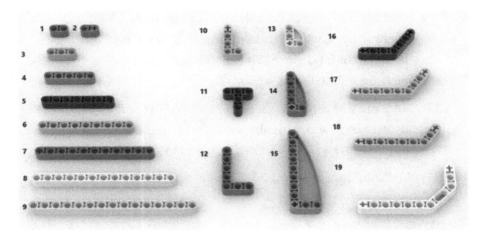

***Figure 1-10.*** *Samples of LEGO Technic beams*

1) Technic 2M beam (43857): As stated earlier, most beams are odd-numbered in their measurement, which is equal to the number of holes, and this is the only even-numbered beam

2) Technic 1 × 2 beam with cross and hole (60483): This 2M beam is has an axle hole, as well as a through hole

3) Technic 3M beam (32523): This is the first of the beams with odd-numbered through-hole numbers, and it increases by 2

4) Technic 5M beam (32316)

5) Technic 7M beam (32524)

6) Technic 9M beam (40490)

7) Technic 11M beam (32525)

8) Technic 13M beam (41239)

9) Technic 15M beam (41239)

10) Technic L-shape 2 × 4 (32140): This is a merging of a two Technic beams to form a right angle, and one of the holes is cross-shaped, for an axle

11) Technic T-beam 3 × 3 (60484): Also a merging of two Technic beams to form a right angle, with no axle holes

12) Technic L-shape 3 × 5 (32526)

13) Technic L-shape ellipse 2 × 3 (71708): This would be a simple 2 × 3 right angle, but the ellipse gives it a certain curvature to it

14) Technic L-shape ellipse 2 × 5 (80286)

15) Technic L-shape ellipse 3 × 9 (3916)

16) Technic angular beam 4 × 4 (32348): This is an angular beam that looks like a merging of two beams at a 53.1-degree angle, with axle holes at each end

17) Technic angular beam 4 × 6 (6629): Two beams also at the same 53.1-degree angle

18) Technic angular beam 3 × 7 (32271): Two beams also at the same 53.1-degree angle

19) Technic double angular beam (32009): This particular beam has two 45-degree angles, so it is essentially a 90-degree angle with a good curve to it

# Levers

Think of the levers as the plates of Technic. Plates are the flat pieces that make up the basic brick in traditional Lego. While it takes three plates to create a basic brick, you will need only two levers of the same length to create a congruent beam.

Levers are handy when you want to reinforce something, but don't want to take up are large amount of space. They also come in 90-degree bends, and these nicely designed ones. They also have sections here devoted to axle-shaped holes.

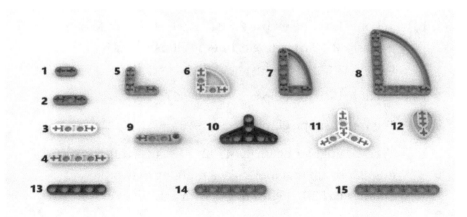

*Figure 1-11.* *Samples of LEGO Technic levers*

1) Technic lever 1 × 2 (41677): This lever has two cross-shaped holes that are 2M in length, only made for securing axles

2) Technic lever 1 × 3 (6632): This type of lever has a cross-shaped hole on each end and a round hole in the middle

3) Technic lever 1 × 4 (32449): A type of lever is larger than the 3M, with two round holes in the middle and axle holes on each end.

4) Technic lever 1 × 5 (11478): This type of lever is larger than the 4M, with three round holes in the middle and axle holes on each end

5) Technic lever 3 × 3 (32056): These are 3M levers fused together at a 90-degree angle, with cross-shaped holes at each of its vertices

6) Technic half beam curve 3 × 3 (32449): This particular lever looks similar to the 3 × 3 and a circular curve joining two ends

7) Technic half beam curve 3 × 5 (32250)

8) Technic half beam curve 5 × 7 (32251)

9) Technic lever 1 × 4 with modified stud connector (2825): This 4M lever has a thicker end on one side

10) Technic triangle 3 × 5 (2905): This particular part has five through holes and two axle holes

11) Technic lever 3 × 120 (44374): This is a propeller-shaped part with three beams measuring 3M at 120-degree angles of one another

12) Technic comb wheel (6575): This is not really shaped like a comb or a wheel, but it does come in handy for securing things

13) Technic 5M half beam (32017): The half beam is essentially a 5M beam split down the middle with five round holes

14) Technic 6M half beam (32063)

15) Technic 7M half beam (32065)

# Axles

Axles first started out as essentially an axle for wheels, and they are made for the plus-shaped through hole. In Technic, they are very handy not only for wheels but also for gears.

The shortest is the two, and sometimes, it comes with notches, and it can be red or black, depending on what set you have. Axles can be a lot of colors, but generally the rule is odd-numbered ones are gray, while even-numbered ones are black. There are other sorts of colors that I have discovered in other Technic sets, though.

There are types that have a stud at the end, and there are types that have a stop, so it won't stick out. Then there are types that have a stop part way through.

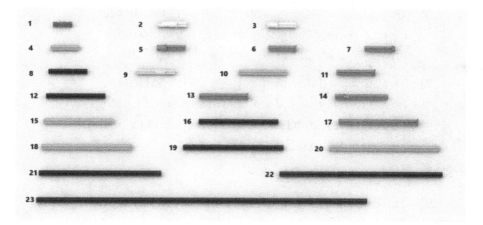

*Figure 1-12.* *Samples of LEGO Technic axles*

1) Technic axle 2M (32062): Axles can come in different colors, but I've seen them primarily in red or black. Usually, the 2M ones are notched, perhaps to make them easier to pry out

2) Technic axle 1M with pin 2M with friction (11214): This particular one has an axle on one end at 1M and a connector pin for the remaining 2M

3) Technic axle 2M with pin without friction (65249): This particular part has an axle for 2M, then a pin without friction, making it easier to rotate when connected

4) Technic axle 3M (4519): While these 3M axles come in many colors, most of the odd-numbered lengths of axles are usually gray in color

5) Technic axle 2M with pin and friction (18651): While 2M of this part is an axle, the rest is a connector pin with friction

25

6) Technic axle 3M with stop (24316): This particular type of 3M axle has a stop on the end, which will ensure that it will not go pass the through hole

7) Technic axle 3M with stud (6587): This 3M axle has a stud on the end which will stop it from going through a through hole, and it is a stud that you can click a traditional LEGO onto

8) Technic axle 3M (3705)

9) Technic axle 4M with center stop (99008): This one has 2M of axle on one side and 1M on the other, with a space in the middle that works like a connector pin

10) Technic axle 5M (32073)

11) Technic axle 4M with stop (87083)

12) Technic axle 6M (3706)

13) Technic axle 5M with stop (15462)

14) Technic axle 5.5M with stop (32209): This is an axle about 5.5 M in length, with a stop 4M through and then the rest being more axle

15) Technic axle 7M (44294)

16) Technic axle 8M (3707)

17) Technic axle 8M with stop (55013)

18) Technic axle 9M (60485)

19) Technic axle 10M (3737)

20)   Technic axle 11M (23948)

21)   Technic axle 12M (3708)

22)   Technic axle 16M (50451)

23)   Technic axle 32M (50450)

# Connector Pegs/Pins and Bushes

As implied in their name, these particular parts are made so that it can join one Technic part to another, whether it be two beams, or other similar Technic parts. They come in many types, and some have axle parts, but the connector peg/pin will snap in.

Some of these connector pegs/pins will have friction, which means that they will spin very easily. The ones with friction will still spin, but not as fast or as easily. These parts can be very small, but they can do quite a lot.

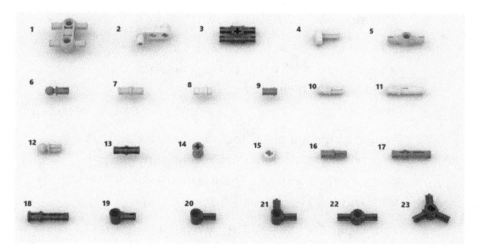

***Figure 1-13.***  *Samples of LEGO Technic connector pegs/pins and bushes*

1) Technic beam 3M with four snaps (48989): This has four connector pegs with round holes on the other and another round hole in between the two connector pegs

2) Technic modified crank pin 1 × 3 (33299): This is a leer with a connector peg on one side and a 1M axle hole on the other side

3) Technic peg double with axle hole (32138): This part has two connector pegs on each side and an axle hole in the middle

4) Technic engine crankshaft (2853): If you insert a 2M axle into one side of a 2M lever, you will essentially have this part, but all in one section

5) Technic peg 3M with center pin hole (87082): Think of a through hole with connector pegs attached on either side, and you have this part

6) Technic peg with tow ball (6628b): This particular part is made to stick into a through hole and then have tow ball, which comes in handy for many situations

7) Technic connector peg without friction (3673): This is a good part to have when connecting any Technic part to another, and since there is no friction, it will spin easily

8) Technic peg 3/4 (32002): This part has a connector peg on one side and a stud on the other

9) Technic peg 1/2 (4274): This is similar to the 3/4 peg, with the stud a lot smaller

10) Technic 1M axle with connector peg without friction (3749): A commonly used part that joins an axle hole with a through hole and allows for some good spinning action

11) Technic 3M peg without friction (32556): This is a connector peg that is 2M on one side and 1M on the other, with a stop in the middle. It is good for all kinds of situations, especially if spinning is involved

12) Technic axle with tow ball (2736): This particular part is made to stick into an axle hole and then have tow ball, which comes in handy for many situations

13) Technic connector peg with friction (2780): This is a good part to have when connecting any Technic part to another, and since there is friction, it will not spin easily

14) Technic bush (3713): This part is made to stick onto an axle, and it is very good at creating a stop on it

15) Technic half bush (4265c): This part is the same as a bush, but half the length

16) Technic 1M axle with connector peg with friction (43093): Another commonly used part that joins an axle hole with a through hole and allows for limited spinning action

17) Technic 3M peg with friction (6558): This is a connector peg that is 2M on one side and 1M on the other, with a stop in the middle

18) Technic peg 3M with stop bush (32054): This is one part that is 2M on one side, with an axle hole on the other side

19)    Technic peg and peg hole (15100): This is a through hole with a connector peg

20)    Technic axle and peg hole (22961): This is a through hole with a 1M axle

21)    Technic peg hole with two perpendicular axles (10197): This is a through hole with two 1M axles that form a 90-degree angle

22)    Technic peg hole with two axles (27940): This is a through hole with a 1M axle on opposite sides

23)    Technic axle connector hub with three axles (57585): This is an axle hole with three 1M axles at 120 angles from each other

# Cross Blocks

Occasionally, you will need to connect a beam, lever, or some other part and have it turned at a 90-degree angle. Fortunately, there are many ways of doing that, and some version of the cross blocks are usually the answer to that problem.

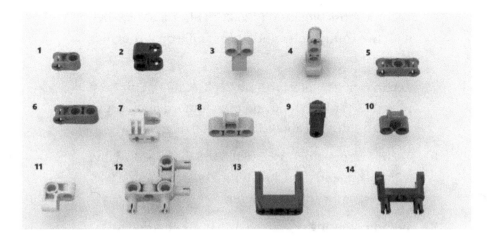

***Figure 1-14.*** *Samples of LEGO Technic cross blocks*

1) Technic cross block 90 degrees (6536): This is a part 2M in length with a round hole in one direction and cross hole facing 90 degrees the other way

2) Technic axle and connector peg perpendicular double split (41678): This part is two round holes and then a cross hole on each side, at 90 degrees below it

3) Technic cross block 2 × 3 (32557): This piece is interesting with two round holes in one direction and two round holes below it at 90 degrees and centered

4) Technic cross block 2 × 4 (98989): Similar to the 2 × 3, the 2 ×4 has two through holes in one direction and three through holes at 90 degrees with one axle hole

5) Technic double cross block (32184): This piece has two axle holes on one side, followed by a through hole centered on the other side

31

6) Technic cross block 3M (42003): This is a 3M beam with two round holes and a cross hole on 90 degrees on the other side

7) Technic cross block form 2 × 2 × 2 (92907): This piece is a through hole and then four axle holes (two on each side) 1M above it, facing 90 degrees away

8) Technic cross block 3 × 2 (63869): This is essentially a 3M beam and then attaching a bush mounted 90 degrees on the top and center

9) Technic steering gear (32068): This is an axle and peg connector made with a through hole, good for steering, as its name implies

10) Technic cross block 1 × 2 (32291): This looks a lot like the cross block 3 × 2, but it is a bush mounted 90 degrees on a 2M beam instead of a 3M beam

11) Technic peg connector perpendicular 2 × 2 bend (44809): This is a unique piece with through holes at a 90-degree angle and a through hole atop of that

12) Technic 3 × 3 perpendicular bend with four pegs (55615): This is a piece that bends at 90 degrees, with two connector pegs on each side

13) Technic peg connector toggle joint smooth double with axle and peg holes (87408): This piece is like a beam with two axle holes on each side, and then there are 3M levers on each side with two through holes each

14) Technic peg connector toggle joint smooth double with two pegs (48496)

# Angle Elements

These pieces are made for holding axles together at certain angles, and the through hole in the middle is an added bonus in case you want to attach them to something.

***Figure 1-15.*** *Samples of LEGO angle elements*

Normally, I had the parts individually numbered, but these pieces, with the exception of the last, are already numbered. In case you can't tell, they are organized from left to right.

1) Technic 0-degree angle element #1 (32013): This is used for rounding off an axle with a through hole at 90 degrees

2) Technic 180-degree angle element #2 (32034): Used for joining two axles together in a straight line, with a through hole in the middle turned at 80 degrees

3) Technic 157.5-degree angle element #3 (32016): The name of this angle element is equivalent to the angle that it is, as is the last three here

4) Technic 135-degree angle element #4 (32192)

5) Technic 112.5-degree angle element #5 (32015)

6)  Technic 90-degree angle element #6 (32013)

7)  Technic axle and peg connector triple (12088): Yes, it is not marked as seven, but it's similar to an angle element, so I counted it, but it can join three axles together at 120 angles in between

# Gears

Much of the features on a Technic model can be done with some application of gears. They are made so that when one spins, so will the other.

The important thing to notice is how much space they take. Also, if one turns another, this will cause the other to turn at equal speed, if the gears are the same size. If the gear that is meshed with is smaller or larger, then this will cause an increase or decrease in its turning speed.

Also, some gears are made so they will turn at a perpendicular angle. There is also the worm gear, made to stay still unless it is spun.

*Figure 1-16.* Samples of LEGO Technic gears

1) Technic conical wheel 12 teeth gear (6589): This gear is flat with 12 teeth and it can spin in a perpendicular fashion with another wheel

2) Technic 20-tooth bevel gear (32198): Similar to the 12 teeth version, it is slightly larger at 20 teeth and can spin in a perpendicular fashion

3) Technic 12-tooth double bevel gear (32270): This can spin like the conical wheels, but is much thicker, and can do perpendicular spins

4) Technic 20 teeth double bevel gear (32269): This is just like the one with 12 teeth, but larger

5) Technic turntable 28 teeth (99009 and 99010): This is actually two pieces combined into one, and it really comes in handy when you need something to swivel

6) Technic 16-tooth gear with clutch (6542): This 16-tooth gear that has a through hole in the middle instead of the usual axle holes

7) Technic 20-tooth bevel gear (87407): This is a 20-tooth gear with a through hole and works in perpendicular fashion

8) Technic 8-tooth gear wheel (3647): This is probably the smallest gear with an axle hole in the middle

9) Technic 16-tooth wheel (4019): This gear is slightly bigger that the 8-tooth one, with a single axle hole in the middle

10) Technic turntable 56 teeth (48168 and 48452): This is another case of two pieces combined into one, and it really comes in handy when you need something to swivel

11) Technic worm gear (4716): This is a gear made to mesh with another round gear above it, and turning this gear will cause the gear to turn. And if this worm gear does not spin, that gear will be locked in place

12) Technic differential 28 teeth (62821b): This piece allows wheels to spin better on a properly made axle, and this one requires three 12-tooth conical wheel gears to function

13) Technic differential 24–16 teeth (6573): Similar to the other differential gear casing, but with an extra gear housing

14) Technic 24-tooth gear wheel (3648): This is similar to the other gear wheels, but it has three cross holes and four round holes

15) Technic angular wheel (32072): This gear works very well in a perpendicular fashion

16) Technic 14-tooth gear thin bevel (4143): It's one of the skinniest gears, with an axle hole in the middle

17) Technic 14-tooth gear thick bevel (69762): This is a very thick gear with a single axle hole in the center

18) Technic 24-tooth clutch gear (60c01): This 24-tooth gear has a single axle hole in the middle

19) Technic gear wheel 40 teeth (3649): This is one very large LEGO piece, with 12 round holes and 5 cross holes

# Racks and Shocks

The racks work with the gears to produce some interesting effects, and they really come in handy when it comes to steering. As for the shocks, these come in handy when they work with the wheels.

I use the racks a lot in this book, as they are handy to create a lot of features such as steering or elevation. The shocks I don't really cover in this book, but I have some models in my other books if you are interested in seeing them in action.

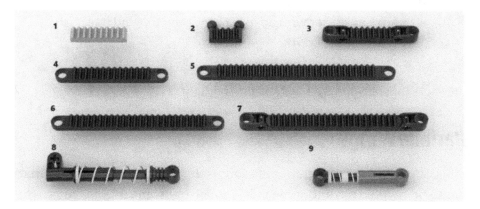

***Figure 1-17.*** *Samples of LEGO racks and shocks*

1) Technic gear rack 1 × 4 (3743): This particular rack could easily work with traditional LEGO bricks as it just snaps on top

2) Technic 1 × 2 gear rack with two tow balls (6574): There is a special trick that can be done here with these particular products to help out with steering

3) Technic gear rack 1 × 7 with axle holes (87761): This particular rack has a through hole on each end and two axle holes as well

4)  Technic gear rack 1 × 8 with holes (6630): Like the other previously mentioned rack, this one only has flat through holes at each end and no axle holes on the side

5)  Technic gear rack 1 × 14 with holes (32185)

6)  Technic gear rack 1 × 12 with holes (32132)

7)  Technic gear rack 1 × 13 with axle holes (64781)

8)  Technic shock absorber 9.5 M (95292c01): This is a shock absorber with an axle hole at the top and has an extra hard spring

9)  Technic shock absorber 6.5 M (731c04): This shock absorber has a hard spring and tight coils

# Panels/Wings

The issue with a lot of Technic creations is that there is a lot of space that has to be covered up, and some of it is small, but some is quite large. I had to divide this section up to three illustrations to highlight how diverse this is.

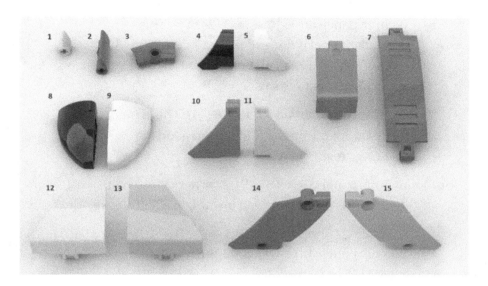

***Figure 1-18.*** *Samples of LEGO Technic panels and wings*

1)  Technic panel curved 2 × 1 × 1 (89679): The smallest of the panels, with an axle hole to attach

2)  Technic panel curved 2 × 3 × 1 (71682): This particular panel is 3M wide and with axle holes on both sides

3)  Technic panel curved 2 × 3 × 1 angled (2457): The panel is angled so it appears to bend in the middle

4)  Technic panel curved #10 3 × 3 tapered right (2403): This is going to be the beginning of wing-shaped panels that have a number put on them (number ten in this case) and have many through holes for attachment

5)  Technic panel curved #9 3 × 3 tapered left (2395): This is the beginning of panels that will be the opposite direction of the last one

6) Technic panel curved 3 × 5 × 3 (24116): This particular panel is flat and beat at a certain angle, resembling a car seat, and often used as that in many LEGO Technic sets

7) Technic panel curved 3 × 13 (18944): This panel is curved slightly in the middle and good for covering areas

8) Technic panel curved 5 × 3 × 2 corner ellipse right (2442): This panel is curved inward, like half a nose of an airplane

9) Technic panel curved 5 × 3 × 2 corner ellipse left (2438)

10) Technic panel curved #62 5 × 4 tapered right (80274)

11) Technic panel curved #63 5 × 4 tapered left (80278)

12) Technic panel curved #70 5 × 4 × 3 tapered right (80271)

13) Technic panel curved #71 5 × 4 × 3 tapered left (80272)

14) Technic panel curved #60 5 × 7 tapered right (80268)

15) Technic panel curved #61 5 × 7 tapered left (80267)

Here are some more panels that are made to be longer sections of wings and fenders as well.

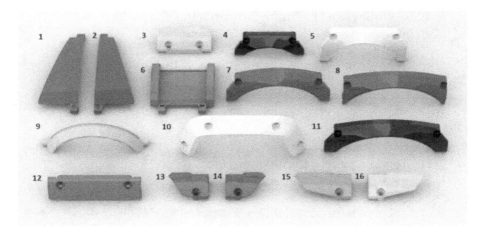

***Figure 1-19.*** *More samples of LEGO Technic wings and panels*

1)   Technic panel curved #50 5 × 13 tapered left (67142)

2)   Technic panel curved #51 5 × 13 tapered
     right (68196)

3)   Technic panel curved 7 × 3 surface (24119): This
     piece is slightly sloped downward

4)   Technic panel car mudguard arched #30 9 × 2 × 3
     (42531): This is one of several mudguard pieces,
     which really come in handy when building cars and
     other vehicles

5)   Technic panel car mudguard arched #32 11 × 2 ×
     5 (2509)

6)   Technic panel curved 8 × 8 × 2 (3251)

7)   Technic panel car mudguard arched #41 13 × 2 ×
     5 (69911)

8) Technic panel car mudguard arched #42 13 × 2 × 5 (80284)

9) Technic panel car mudguard arched 13 × 2 × 5 (71689)

10) Technic panel car mudguard arched 15 × 2 × 7 (46882)

11) Technic panel car mudguard arched #40 15 × 2 × 5 (67141)

12) Technic panel curved 11 × 3 surface (62531)

13) Technic panel #1 side A (87080)

14) Technic panel #2 side B (87086)

15) Technic panel #3 side A (64683)

16) Technic panel #4 side B (64391)

This next section of panels has more wing-shaped panels and some flat ones at that.

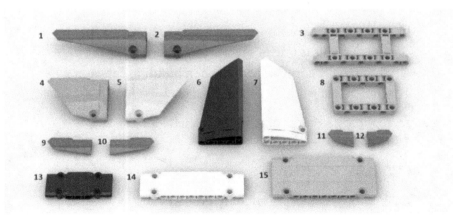

***Figure 1-20.*** *Even more samples of LEGO Technic wings and panels*

1)  Technic panel fairing #5 side A (64681)

2)  Technic panel fairing #6 side B (64393)

3)  Technic modified frame 5 × 11 (64178): This panel is
    a frame of beams, with through holes all around it

4)  Technic panel fairing #13 side A (64394)

5)  Technic panel fairing #14 side B (64680)

6)  Technic panel fairing #17 side A (64392)

7)  Technic panel fairing #18 side B (64682)

8)  Technic modified frame 5 × 7 (64179)

9)  Technic panel fairing #22 side A (11947)

10) Technic panel fairing #21 side B (11946)

11) Technic panel fairing #7 side A (2387)

12) Technic panel fairing #8 side B (2389)

13) Technic panel plate 3 × 7 × 1 (71709): This is a flat
    solid panel, which looks very good to fill in space on
    a LEGO Technic creation

14) Technic panel plate 3 × 11 × 1 (15458)

15) Technic panel plate 11 × 5 × 1 (64782)

# Flexible Hose

Every once in a while, you need a way to show curves on a Technic model.
One good way is by using flexible hose to bend it in the direction you need
it to go. This is where these hoses come in, as they can bend very easily.

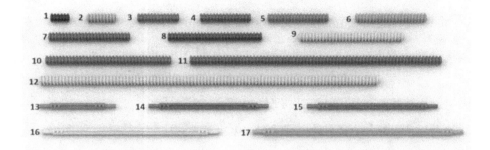

**Figure 1-21.** *Samples of LEGO Technic flexible hose*

1) Technic ribbed hose 2M (78c02): The smallest of the flexible hose, but its small size makes it not worthy of doing a lot of bends. Like most of the ribbed flexible hose, it can house an axle of 2M

2) Technic ribbed hose 3M (78c03)

3) Technic ribbed hose 4M (78c04)

4) Technic ribbed hose 5M (78c05)

5) Technic ribbed hose 6M (78c06)

6) Technic ribbed hose 7M (78c07)

7) Technic ribbed hose 8M (78c08)

8) Technic ribbed hose 9M (78c09)

9) Technic ribbed hose 10M (78c10)

10) Technic ribbed hose 12M (78c12)

11) Technic ribbed hose 24M (78c24)

12) Technic ribbed hose 31M (78c31)

13) Technic soft axle 7M (32580): This particular hose is thinner than the ribbed hose and is more flexible as a result

14) Technic soft axle 11M (32199)

15) Technic soft axle 12M (32200)

16) Technic soft axle 16M (32202)

17) Technic soft axle 19M (32235)

# Wheels and Tires

Of course, if you are going to make any vehicle, and this book has instructions for many of them, you are going to need to put some wheels on it. In addition to round wheels, it is also possible to put on treads, which isn't really something that I discuss in this book, but I wanted you to know the option is available.

*Figure 1-22.* *Samples of LEGO wheels*

1) Technic wedge belt wheel, pulley (4185)

2) Technic tread sprocket wheel large (57519)

3) Technic tread sprocket wheel extra large (42529)

4) Technic link tread (3873)

5) Technic link tread wide with two pin holes (57518)

6) Technic link tread extra wide with two pin holes (69910)

7) Wheel 11 mm 6mm with 8 "Y" spokes and black tire (93595c01)

8) Wheel 15 mm city motorcycle with 21 black tire (50862c01)

9) Wheel 30 mm with black tire 43.2 × 14 offset tread (56904c01)

10) Wheel 30.4 mm × 20 mm with no pin holes with black tire 43.2 (56145c01)

11) Wheel 36.8 mm × 26 mm VR with axle hole with black tire 49.6 × 28 VR (22253c01)

12) Wheel 36.8 mm × 26 mm VR with axle hole with black tire 49.6 × 28 VR (6594c02)

13) Wheel 41 mm snap thin tread with black tire 41 mm directional tread (32247c01)

14) Wheel 61.6 mm × 13.6 mm motorcycle with black tire 81.6 × 15 motorcycle (2903c01)

15) Wheel 62.3 mm × 42 mm Technic racing large with black tire 81.6 × 44 ZR (23800c01)

16) Wheel 75 mm × 17 mm motorcycle with black tire 94.2 mm × 2mm motorcycle (88517c01)

# Miscellaneous

Like I have said before on certain individual categories of Technic pieces, this is not meant to be an exhaustive list, and so I put in other pieces here as examples of pieces that I can't really categorize.

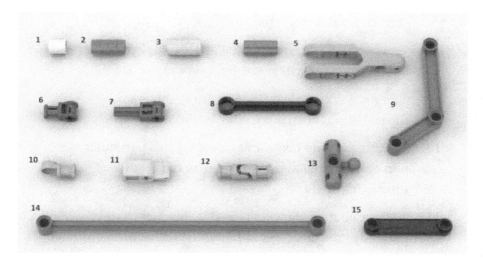

***Figure 1-23.*** *Samples of LEGO miscellaneous pieces*

1) Technic 1 × 1 spacer (18654): The smallest of tubes at 1M, it can house an axle length of 1M

2) Technic axle connector 2M, ridged (6538a): Designed to connect two axles together at each end and ridged for better grip

3) Technic tube 2M (75535): This 2M tube can house a 2M axle length or have a connector peg at each end

4) Technic axle connector 2M, smooth (6538c)

5) Technic steering arm 6 × 2 with tow ball (57515): This is used for steering

6) Technic axle connector with axle hole (32039): This is an axle hole with another axle hole at a 90-degree angle

7) Technic axle 2M with reverse handle axle connector (6553): Think of a 2M axle attached to an axle connector, and this is the part

8) Technic 1 × 6 with stoppers (2739b): This part is a 6M bar with a place for tow balls on each end

9) Technic 1 × 9 bent 6-4 (64451): This bar has some through holes at an interesting angle

10) Technic axle and peg connector (44): This particular part can join together with others to create an interesting angle

11) Technic changeover catch (6641): This part comes in handy for shifting gears, which we will cover at another time

12) Technic universal joint 3M (62520c01): This part can join two axles together and will enable them to turn at certain angles

13) Technic steering arm with through hole and tow ball (6571): This is another piece that works well for steering

14) Technic link 1 × 16 (2637)

15) Technic link 1 × 5 (30397)

# Conclusion

LEGO Technic is essentially a way to make larger-scale models, as well as grant them features. It works using LEGO Technic pieces that are, in many ways, very different from traditional LEGO pieces, but can still work together.

Considering how expensive LEGO sets can be, you might be able to save money on purchasing LEGO Technic pieces by going to online auctions for bulk purchases of LEGO pieces, but you might find that LEGO Technic could come up short. Therefore, I recommend BrickLink if you need certain individual LEGO Technic pieces.

Once you have the LEGO Technic pieces that you will need, I recommend organizing them by function, with the categories that I showed earlier. This will make building more efficient and less time-consuming. Speaking of building, let's get into a great creation that will be full of features.

# CHAPTER 2

# A Solid Base of Features

Okay, now that you have all your pieces, it is time to get to building. Of course, you might want to ask yourself if you can even do what you want. I would suggest that you take the time to plan it out. This is actually what is going to be the subject of this chapter, and by the end of it, you will be able to construct a base for a LEGO Technic car.

## Building with LEGO in a Virtual World

By now, you have hopefully been able to assemble the basics of a Technic kit. By that, I mean a good collection of pieces that I discussed in Chapter 1. Yet even if you can't find any pieces anywhere, what if there was a place where you could find any piece of any kind, in any color you want?

Fortunately, this technology exists today and it is absolutely free. Granted, you might not be able to hold a piece in your hand, nor your model, but you will be able to see what it looks like. Not only that, you will be able to see if it is even possible to build it.

© Mark Rollins 2024
M. Rollins, *The Ultimate LEGO Technic Book*, Maker Innovations Series,
https://doi.org/10.1007/979-8-8688-0793-0_2

# Stud.io

I highly recommend downloading the latest version of stud.io which can be found at https://www.bricklink.com/v3/studio/download.page. I had a bit of an issue when I downloaded it for the first time, so I recommend that you find the latest version if that aforementioned URL didn't work. From the very beginning, there is a great tutorial, and it was enough to show how to select a piece and then manipulate it in real time.

The advantage of Stud.io is that you can select a piece from many categories, and I designed the categories in Chapter 1 of this book to correspond to the categories on Stud.io. Underneath that section, you can search the parts for what piece that you need, but I had to admit that unless you know the official name or number, you might have better results doing a visual search.

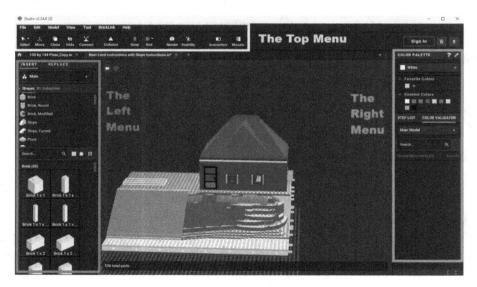

*Figure 2-1.* *Stud.io screenshot and the menus for control*

I have to admit that I really like the interface of Stud.io. I have used other LEGO drawing programs like LDraw and LeoCAD for my other books, and I found them to be somewhat taxing. Stud.io reminds me a lot of Lego Digital Designer, which is a program that LEGO used to have available where you just select a brick and set it in 3D space.

Unfortunately, there are times where Stud.io doesn't quite work as well as it should, especially if you are working on something where there are a lot of bricks. Oftentimes, the AI in Stud.io thinks you are trying to put a piece in a place where you don't want it to go, and it won't select the area where you do want it to go. Fortunately, there are ways around this, which I will discuss further.

## The Menu on the Left

You will notice that once a brick is selected, you can use the arrow keys to determine its direction and position, and it will flip it or turn it at 90 degrees. If you want to do some other angle, you can select the rotation tool, and that will allow you to turn it at a very precise angle, and I have demonstrations of this in this chapter and others.

While I'm on the subject of manipulating a piece, you can also click on the Move tool, which will allow you to move a brick in a limited space in the x axis, y axis, or z axis. You can use this tool in places in cases where the Stud.io AI won't allow you to put a brick in a certain place. Or at least not without great difficulty, so the Move tool really helps limit the piece mobility so you can get it in place.

You will notice that you can select "Replace," which is a handy tool to use while you are building. You will have to select the brick that you are working on, and it will only suggest bricks that take up the same area. For example, if you select a 2 × 4 brick, it will give you suggestions that include a 2 × 4 plate, 2 × 4 slope, or any other brick that takes up the same area, but not necessarily the same volume.

There is also a button here that can change all the pieces to a certain color, and you can see that you can see that pieces come in all the colors of the rainbow and then some. In fact, it is quite possible that LEGO does not even make that shape in that color, something you will need to think about if you want to bring your creation to life. In fact, this would be a good time for me to say that I use bricks with colors that LEGO does not make as illustrations in this book.

There is also an option for toggling Decorated Bricks on and off. Decorated Bricks is exactly what it sounds like, a LEGO piece that has some kind of permanent writing or picture. I didn't cover Decorated Bricks at all in Chapter 1 because I wanted to discuss pieces in their most blank form, but LEGO, with its thousands of sets throughout the past decades, has had quite many Decorated Bricks. I'm very certain the last chapter would have been multiplied greatly if I included every Decorated Brick that LEGO has created. As an added note, Decorated Bricks are different from the stickers that LEGO has in some of their sets, which I don't think are really possible to apply with Stud.io.

There is another button here that will change the layout of the piece menu so you can see what you have to work with in a column that is 1, 2, or 3 pieces wide. I have to admit that I had some issues with this, because the smaller a piece is on the screen, the harder it is to recognize.

## The Menu on the Right

The default menu on the right is set up for the colors of the piece and a way to color any piece selected with whatever color that you want. Like I said before, you can color a piece with a color that LEGO doesn't make. You will notice that pieces of a certain color will have exclamation marks on them, which means that you won't be able to find a piece of that shape available in that color.

This menu also has a place to set up steps. Think of it as steps in a LEGO instruction booklet, and it comes in handy when you are creating any project from the ground up. Of course, you can always create something from the ground down, like you can create a roof and work your way down.

If you want to create instructions for yourself, like the ones that I have in my books, I highly recommend using the step tool. The issue is that you need to be conscious of it, because the Step List will only record whatever steps that you use as you select your pieces.

So as you build, hit "Add Step," and this will create a place for the pieces you will use, and then keep going. You can right click each step and move the pieces around, delete them, or even hide them, which I will explain later.

There is also a Color Validator, a terrific tool that allows for some easy editing in case you have a piece that is in a color that LEGO does not produce. You can even have Stud.io do an autocorrect on it to give it a color that LEGO does have of its type. For example, I had a Brick Modified 2 × 4 × 2 with holes on the sides that was in purple, but the Color Validator noted that the piece is available in black and made the correction.

## The Top Menu

Select allows you to highlight a certain piece, and hitting CTRL will highlight another piece. From there, you can use the Rotation and Move Tool and other things.

You can also select a piece by color, like if you want to select all the blue bricks, you can do that, and you can do whatever you want with them. You can even select a piece by type and color, not to mention by connection.

Hinge allows you to select a piece and then change the specific angle on it. It can be manipulated in three dimensions, and this is how you can make hinge pieces work for you. We briefly discussed in Chapter 1 how the hinge pieces work and how to adjust the angles of them.

The Clone allows a piece to be immediately duplicated, and it will appear directly atop of that.

Hide will hide a piece. The reason you would want to do that is because there are times where you will want to put a piece somewhere, but the AI doesn't know how to process it. So you can try dragging it to a spot, and it won't go where you want it to. It helps to hide pieces around that piece, and you will have an easier time putting it in place. If a brick is hidden, it will show on the screen, and it is possible to reveal them all at the touch of a button.

Connect is an excellent tool for just linking bricks. There are going to be times where the AI can't figure out what you are trying to do with a certain brick, like if you can't fit one in where it needs to go. For this, I recommend just clicking the place where you want the first brick and then clicking where it needs to go.

There is also a Collision button that, when engaged, will allow you to see if parts will fit together. Stud.io will often allow you to put pieces in places where they would not regularly fit, which can be problematic if you are trying to build a real-life model.

The Snap button is usually defaulted to "On," and you will discover that when it is off, the piece will go literally wherever. However, with the Snap mode engaged, pieces will drag and then stick where they need to.

For the Grid function, this will regulate how far a piece will move with the directional controls. You can move it one stud at a time, or with smaller movements. By the way, you can move a selected piece with the W, A, S, and D keys.

Render is where you can take your creation and really put it in a great image. You will find that a lot of the illustrations in this book have been created with Render, and I am surprised at the photo-realism that is possible.

Stability is where you will start to get a warning about how safe is your creation. Anything that looks very questionable is taken into account, and it will warn you by highlighting it in red.

Instruction will take your steps and put them in a form like a traditional LEGO set of instructions.

Mosaic is an interesting tool that allows you to upload an image and then make it so it is a mosaic, which is a really fantastic tool that we won't really cover in this book.

# Setting Up a Plan

These things are very important in setting up some kind of great blueprint, but I can understand if you feel better just sitting and planning it out. You can go online, and you can find many LEGO builders who have created something very amazing out of LEGO Technic.

I have heard stories of how many weeks, months, or even years creations like that can take. I have to admit that I am nowhere near that level, honestly, and I will also admit that it might take a while before you ever get to that level.

The important thing is that you have to give it a try, and so I will recommend making some kind of plan before you commit to a project that might cost you a lot in LEGO pieces, or take up valuable free time that you need to spend with your family or on your job.

When it comes to LEGO Technic, the possibilities are limitless and rather limited. Technic is great for when you want to make very advanced vehicles, and I would recommend starting out with a car. It's what I'm going to spend a great majority of this chapter talking about, along with instructions.

I will tell you that this car body that I am building is going to do two things: (1) it has a front steering mechanism and (2) it has an engine with pistons. I have to admit that this is really going back to the original

Lego Go-Kart set 948 that was not only one of the first, but it was the first Technic or LEGO Expert sets that I owned. I am not certain if I deliberately did this, or it just happened to be this way, but I am pleased with the result, and I hope that you are too.

Just to let you know, the car body that I am going to show you in the chapter is going to be very plain, and it won't be the most feature-rich. Yes, there will be later models in this book that will be far more advanced than the one that I will show you here, but I want to show you a gradual progression. After all, there is a reason why kindergarten teachers don't just give you a calculator do solve $2 + 2 = 4$, because it is important that learners understand the concept and can apply it to bigger things.

Originally, when I started this chapter, I was going to show how to build whatever car that you want, like the basic shell or body of one, and then drape it over this model. Of course, all cars are not the same, and you can't just take off the shell of a car and have the same thing underneath, it just doesn't work that way, and it is good that it doesn't. All cars have a distinct width and engine type, which will affect their individual performance.

So yes, I decided to start with the inside first and reversed the order of how I originally wanted to do these chapters. I think I am better off for it, and I'm going to give a step-by-step instruction on what to do for a basic starter kit for a LEGO Technic car.

# The Engine

I'm going to start with this engine, which I have determined to be a V6, for reasons that I will specify in the next chapter. I am going to say that this engine is going to be in the back of the car, which is not really like most cars. However, it will have several pistons that go up and down once the wheels turn.

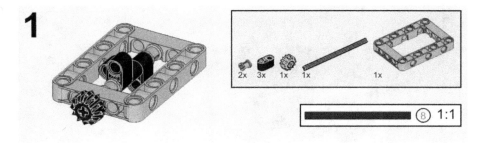

***Figure 2-2.*** *Stick the 8M axle through the 5 × 7 panel with the 2M beam with axle holes, bushes, and the 12-tooth gear double bevel*

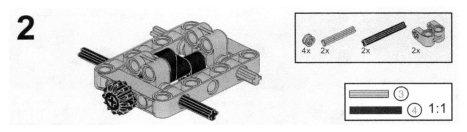

***Figure 2-3.*** *Use the 3M and 4M axles to secure the axle and pin connector perpendicular split with the half bushes*

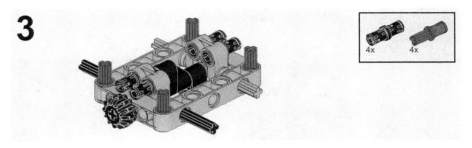

***Figure 2-4.*** *Put on the connector pegs with the connector peg/cross axles*

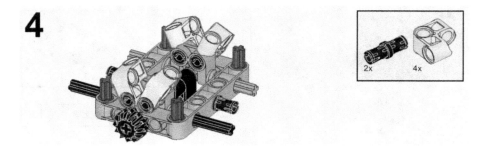

**Figure 2-5.** *Put on the pin connector perpendicular 2 × 2 bent with connector pegs*

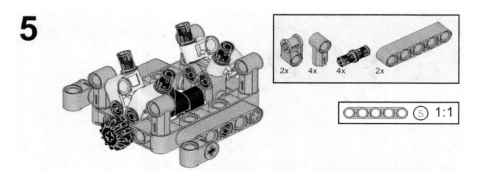

**Figure 2-6.** *Put on the 5M beams and 90-degree cross blocks, along with the #1 angle connector and connector pegs*

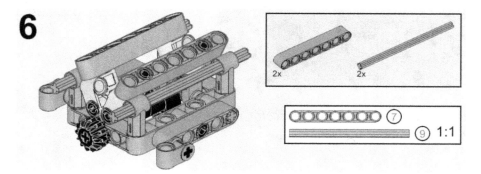

**Figure 2-7.** *Put on the 7M beam and the 9M axles*

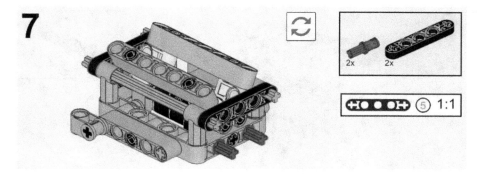

*Figure 2-8.* Put on the 5M levers and the connector peg/cross axles

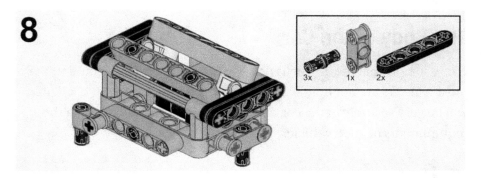

*Figure 2-9.* Put on the 5M levers with the double cross blocks and connector pegs

**9**

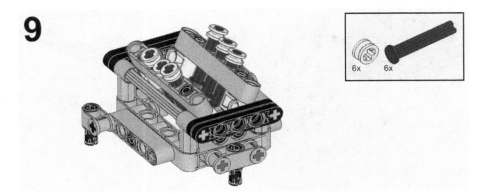

*Figure 2-10.* *Put on the 3M axles with stops and the half bushes*

# The Body of the Car

Okay, so now that the engine is done, let's build the body around it. Yes, most real cars are not built like this, but this is one way to do this. This will be very securely in the car, and having a strong body is one of the requirements of good vehicle.

**10**

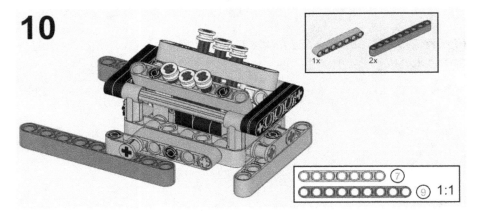

*Figure 2-11.* *Put on the 7M and 9M beams*

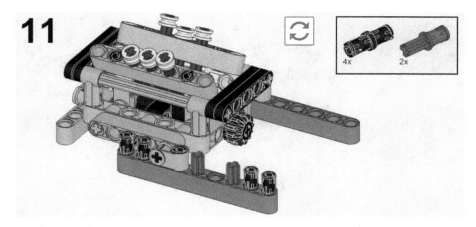

*Figure 2-12.* *Put on the connector pegs and connector peg/cross axles*

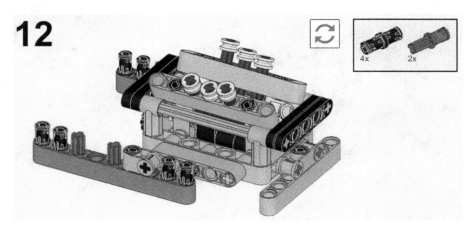

*Figure 2-13.* *Time to put on connector pegs with the connector peg/ cross axles*

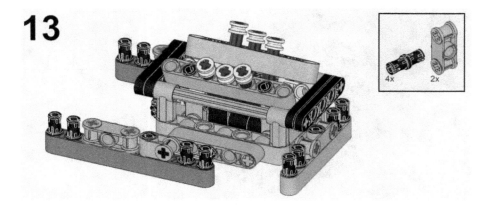

***Figure 2-14.*** *Put on the connector pegs and the double cross blocks*

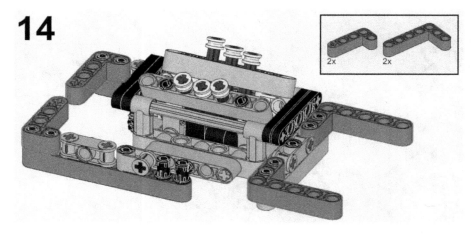

***Figure 2-15.*** *Put on the 2 × 4 and 3 × 5 beams*

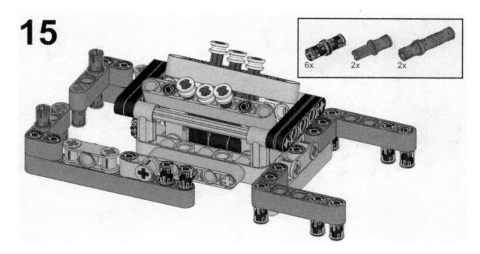

*Figure 2-16.* *Put on the connector pegs, the connector peg/cross axles, and 3M connector pegs*

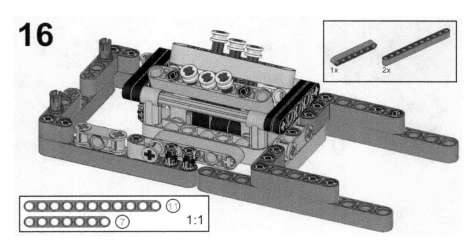

*Figure 2-17.* *Put on the 7M beam and 11M beams*

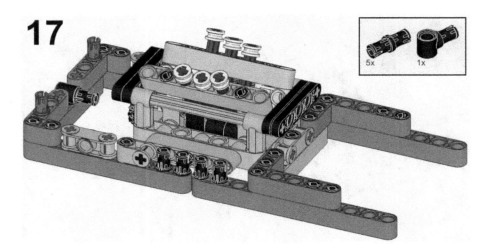

*Figure 2-18.* Put on the connector pegs and the connector peg with pin hole

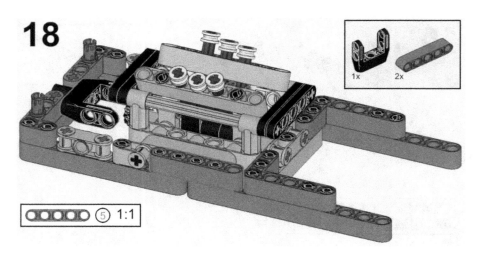

*Figure 2-19.* Put on the 5M beams and the pin connector toggle joint smooth double with axle and pin holes

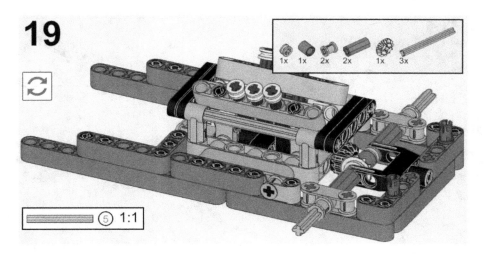

***Figure 2-20.*** *Put on the 5M axles, the 1M tube, the 2M axle connectors, half bushes, bushes, and the gear 12-tooth bevel*

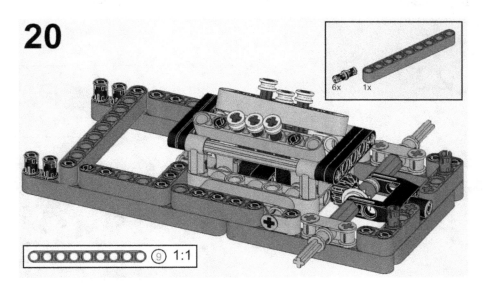

***Figure 2-21.*** *Put on the 9M beam with the connector pegs*

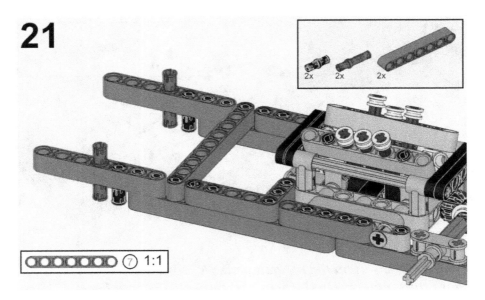

*Figure 2-22. Put on the 7M beams, the 3M connector pegs, and the other connector pegs too*

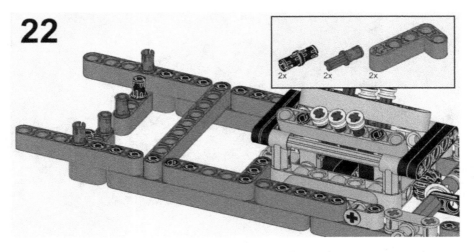

*Figure 2-23. Put on the 2 × 4 beam, as well as the connector pegs with connector peg/cross axles*

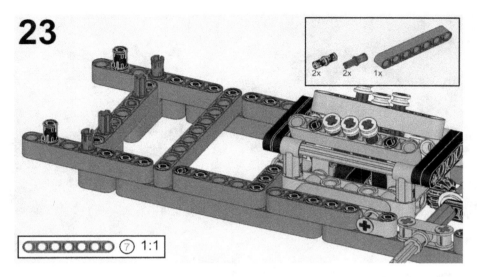

***Figure 2-24.*** *Put on the 7M beam and the connector pegs with connector peg/cross axles*

## The Steering Mechanism

Now, this is going to be one of those Technic constructions that can do a lot of things, and one of them is that it will steer. In order to do that, you have to make a place to have a wheel.

You're also going to have to make a way so that the steering wheel will actually turn the wheels when it is turned. Now, that is the tricky part. Fortunately, it is nothing that some kind of rack-and-pinion mechanism can't fix.

This is just one way to do this, and believe it or not, I had the rack on wrong in the first draft, and the car turned the wrong way. Seriously, left became right and vice versa. I have since fixed it so it works correctly.

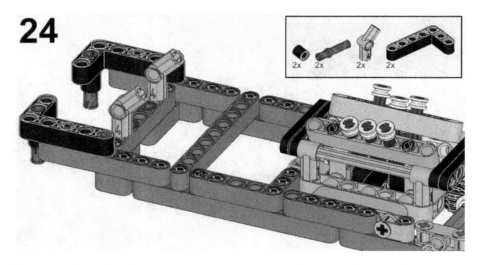

**Figure 2-25.** *Use the #4 angle connectors, the 3 × 5 beams, the 3M connector pegs, and 1M tubes*

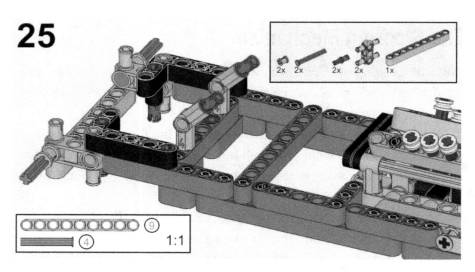

**Figure 2-26.** *Use the pin connector perpendicular 3M with four pins with the connector peg cross axles, the 4M axles (with stop), bushes, and the 9M beam*

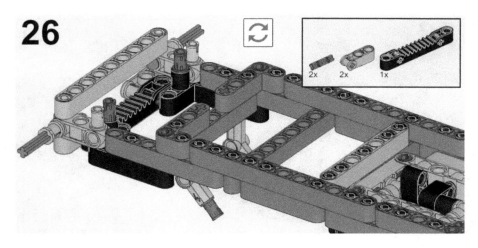

*Figure 2-27.* Use the 2M axles, 3M cross block with axle, and 7M rack

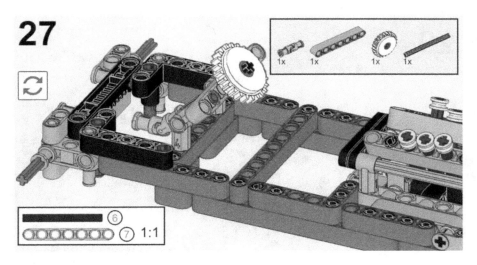

*Figure 2-28.* Put on the universal joint 3M, 7M rack, 6M axle, and the gear

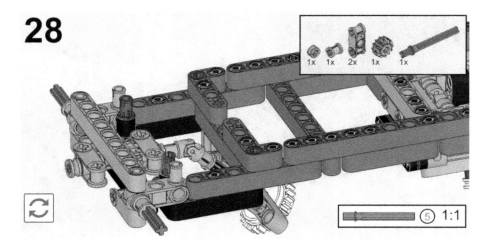

**Figure 2-29.** *Put on the double cross blocks, bushes, the 12-tooth bevel gear, and the axle*

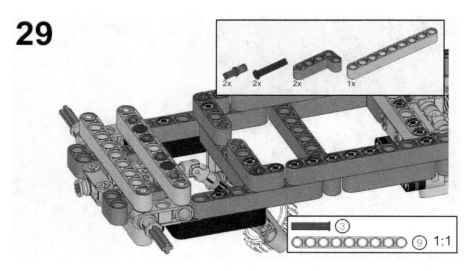

**Figure 2-30.** *Put on the 9M beam, along with the 2 × 4 beams, and the 3M axles with stops and the connector peg/cross axles*

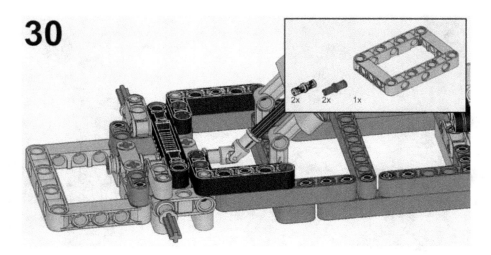

*Figure 2-31.* *Put on the 5 × 7 beam and the connector pegs and connector peg/cross axles*

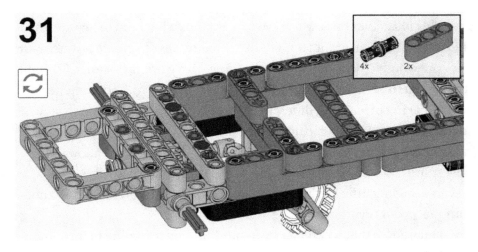

*Figure 2-32.* *Put on the 3M beams, along with the connector pegs*

**32**

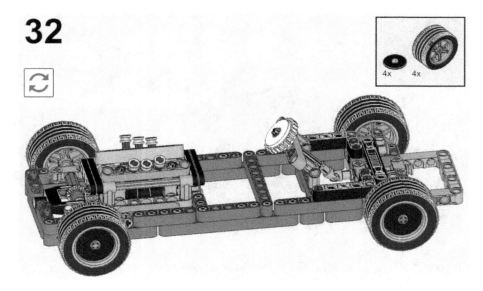

*Figure 2-33.* *For the final step, put on the wheels and rims*

This particular base will serve you as far as what kind of features that LEGO Technic will grant you. There are many ways to create a system for steering your vehicle, as well as an engine with working pistons. I should thank YouTuber Bricks Master Builders for the help with this engine.

Speaking of learning different ways of building, I recommend viewing digital scans of LEGO instructions from older LEGO sets, so you can get a good grasp of how to create all kinds of LEGO Technic creations with awesome features. From there, you can learn to improvise and even reverse engineer the creation to make improvements on it, so it becomes uniquely your own.

I guarantee that when you start building, you are going to hit some kind of snag or something that you can't figure out. There will be times where you will be doing everything you can think of doing for it, only to find that you are still back at square one. If you do get to that point,

I don't recommend continuing to push building or you might just get more frustrated. Sometimes, it is necessary to stop for a while, and then you can start again. I found that usually helps.

Another thing that helps is coming up with some kind of a plan, as that will truly keep you working. I believe that I have discussed how some of these constructions are limited by building in 3D, as you can effectively create a structure that would not stand in real life. When you are building, it is good to start, but if you get stuck, try and plan out the next step in 3D and go from there. Speaking of going from there, we need to go to the next step, right after we wrap up this chapter, of course.

# Conclusion

When it comes to creating Technic creations, the most obvious build is some kind of car. If you are going to build a car, then you might as well make it as feature-rich as possible, which is why I would recommend a basic setup with a steering function as well as a working engine with pistons.

I have included a section here to show how to do a basic start-up base for a Technic car, but if you want to make adjustments, that is possible. This is why I highly recommend downloading Stud.io, so you can try this out for yourself, building a base that you want to build.

With an idea of what you want to build and the virtual program, there is a lot that can be done with LEGO Technic. However, once you have this base with steering and an engine, you want to make the body of the car, in as good of a shape as you can with LEGO.

# CHAPTER 3

# Constructing a LEGO Technic Car Body

All right, now that you have made a base and some steering and engine, so it is time to put a top on, and by "top," I mean the actual auto body. Now, I purposely built the "bottom" in Chapter 2 to essentially serve as the foundation for any car that you wish to build, within reason. After all, this wouldn't be good for a semi or a stretch limo because of the length and number of wheels, but you get the idea. The purpose of this chapter is to show how to make a body of a car, whichever one that you would like.

So, I could have done any car as a demonstration, but I discovered that LEGO has done much of the cooler cars like the Lamborghini and any other fancy sports car that you want to name. A friend of mine suggested I do something like a Dodge Charger, and I decided to do that.

One day, when I was out walking my dog, I passed a car sales lot, and I saw a Dodge Charger SXT 2019, and I took it as confirmation. I started taking pictures of it with my smartphone, and it was really awkward for me to explain to the salesman that I wasn't interested in purchasing it. What I wanted to do was get pics of it at certain angles so I could imitate the bodywork in LEGO Technic.

© Mark Rollins 2024
M. Rollins, *The Ultimate LEGO Technic Book*, Maker Innovations Series,
https://doi.org/10.1007/979-8-8688-0793-0_3

*Figure 3-1.* *Pics of a Dodge Charger SXT, to be used for a LEGO Technic project*

I recommend that if you want to create a LEGO Technic project that is a representation of some real-life vehicle, then you should start by taking pictures of your inspiration.

# LEGO Technic Bodywork

Just to let you know, there was a time when creating a LEGO Technic model left the basic structure looking rather for lack of a better term, naked. That is, there would often be the framework and body of the vehicle, but not really any particular framework of the body.

The issue with a lot of LEGO creations is they don't handle curves very well, because they are by their very nature very square. I'm going to estimate that this is the reason why LEGO Technic moved to curved beams in the mid-2000s, leaving the stud-ridden plates and bricks with the through holes behind, with some exceptions.

Recently, there has been a shift to create vehicles that have a lot of curves to them, and part of that is aided by the panels. While pieces like these might appear to be used as wings (and work well in that regard), it is possible to put a few panels together to create something like a curved front of a car. There are also pieces that are mudguards specifically made for being fenders, so it is smart to work around that. That is, create a model with a scale that allows for the use of these parts.

This next section will discuss how to use such pieces to create the framework of a car, specifically the aforementioned Dodge Charger SXT, starting with something familiar from Chapter 2.

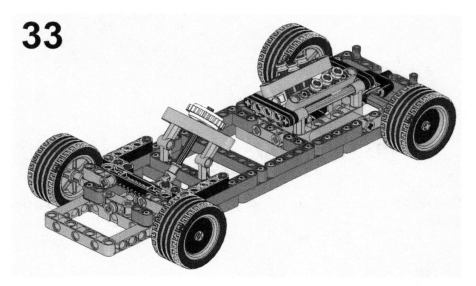

**33**

***Figure 3-2.*** *If you haven't done so already, go ahead and follow the instructions to create this feature-rich foundation for your Dodge Charger SXT body*

You can make this car any color that you want, but I decided to go with red because I found the parts I needed were all available in this color, with one exception. At least, this is what the Color Validator on Stud.io told me.

# 34

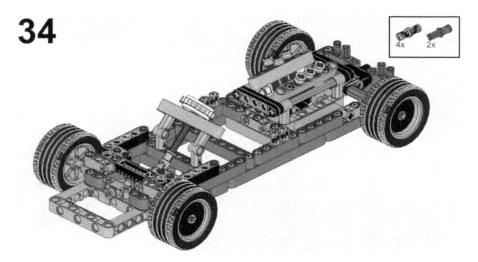

*Figure 3-3.* *Put on the connector pegs and connector peg/cross axles as shown*

# 35

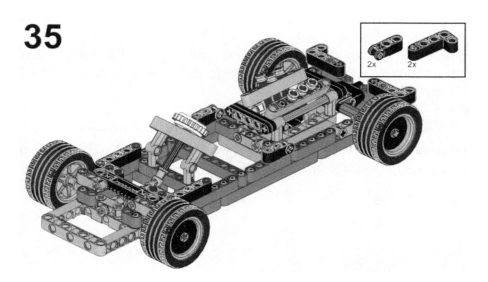

*Figure 3-4.* *Insert the 3M cross blocks with axle and the 2 × 4 beams*

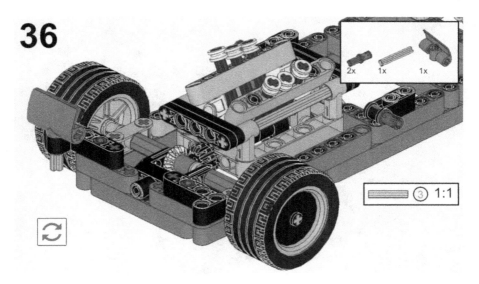

***Figure 3-5.*** *Put on the connector peg/cross axles, and then put on the Technic panel curved 2 × 3 × 1 with the 3M axle*

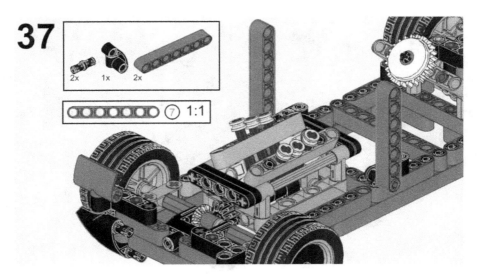

***Figure 3-6.*** *Put on the Technic panel curved #9 3 × 3 tapered left, with the connector pegs, and then put on the 7M beams*

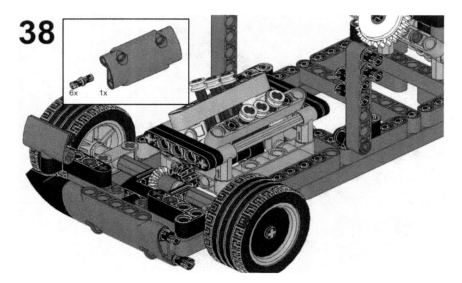

*Figure 3-7.* *Put on the panel curved 7 × 3 with two peg holes and the connector pegs on the 7M beam*

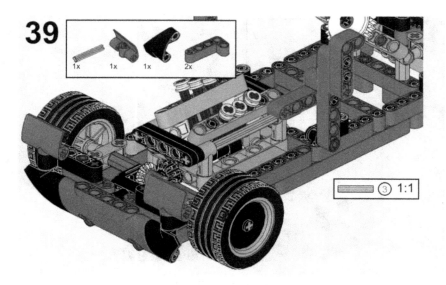

*Figure 3-8.* *Put on the two 2 × 4 beams, the 3M axle with panel curved 2 × 3 × 1 and the panel curved #10 3 × 3 tapered right*

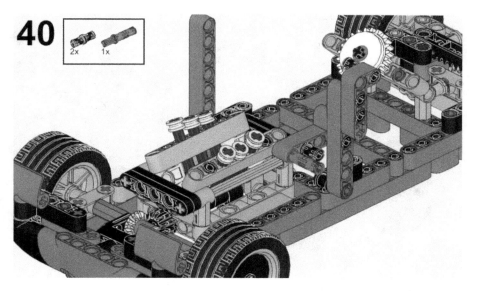

*Figure 3-9.* *Put on the connector pegs and the axle 1M with 2M pin*

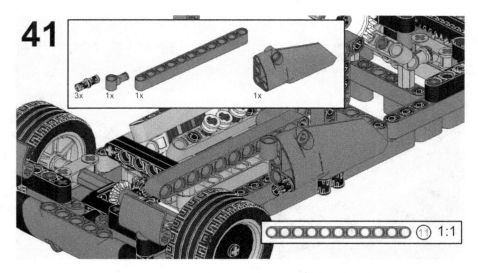

*Figure 3-10.* *Put on the 11M beam, the panel fairing #3, the pin with friction ridges and hole, and then the connector pegs*

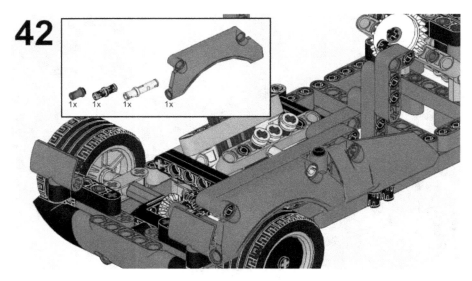

***Figure 3-11.*** *Put on the connector peg, and insert the panel car mudguard arched #30 9 × 2 × 3, with the 3M connector peg without friction ridges and pin 1/2*

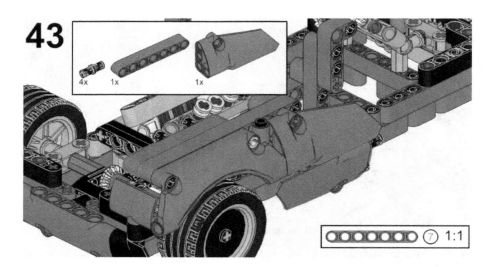

***Figure 3-12.*** *Insert the 7M beam and then the panel fairing #3 with the four connector pegs*

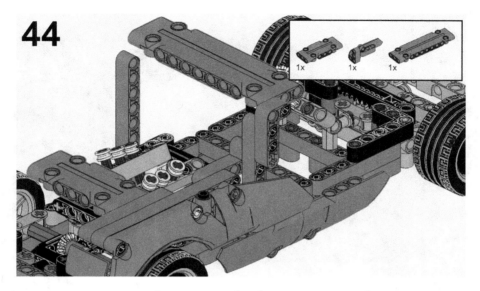

**Figure 3-13.** *Put on the two panels, the 3 × 11 × 1 and 3 × 7 × 1, and then put on the panel fairing #4 on the bottom*

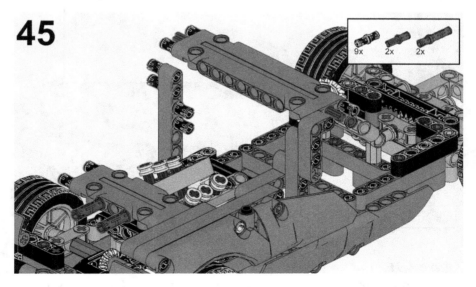

**Figure 3-14.** *Put on the connector pegs, the 3M connector pegs, and the connector pegs/cross axles*

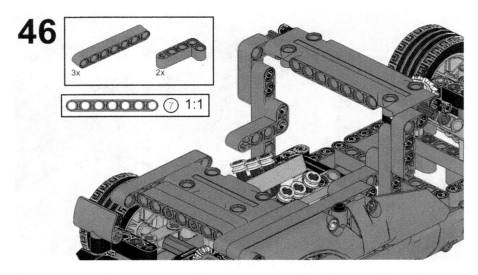

***Figure 3-15.*** *Put on three 7M beams, as well as the two 2 × 4 beams*

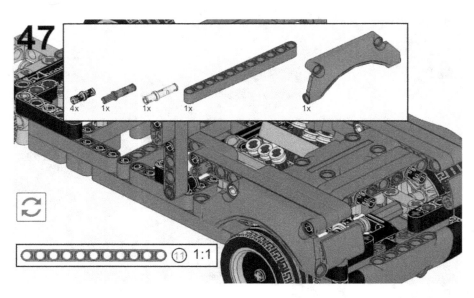

***Figure 3-16.*** *Put on the connector pegs, the axle 1M with 2M pin, the 3M connector peg without friction, then the 11M beam, and #30 mudguard*

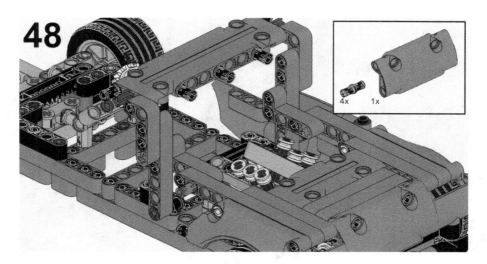

*Figure 3-17.* *Put on the connector pegs and the panel curved 7 × 3 with two pin holes*

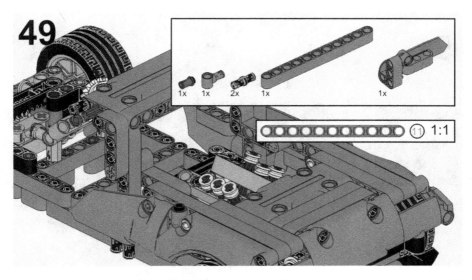

*Figure 3-18.* *Put on the 11M beam, the pin with pin hole, the pin 1/2, the connector pegs, and the panel fairing #4*

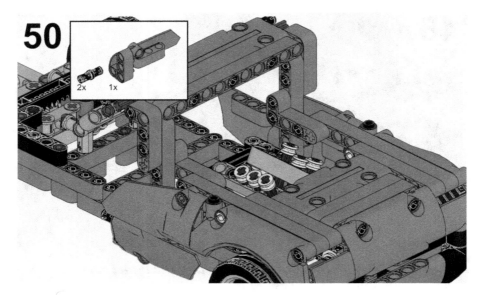

**Figure 3-19.** *Put on another panel fairing #4 and the connector pegs*

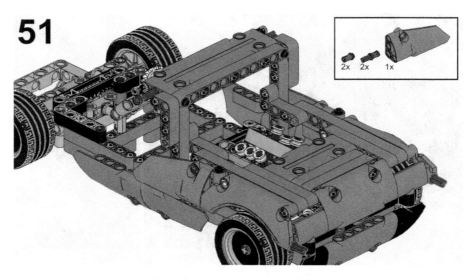

**Figure 3-20.** *Put on the 1/2 pins, the connector peg/cross axles, and the panel fairing #3*

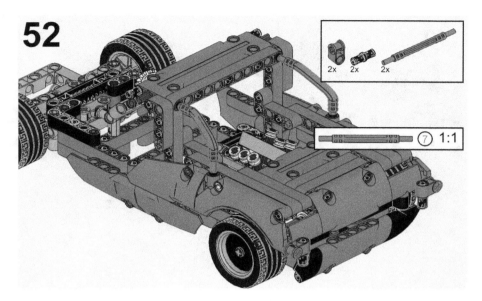

***Figure 3-21.*** *Put on the 90-degree cross blocks, the connector pegs, and the hose, soft axle 7M*

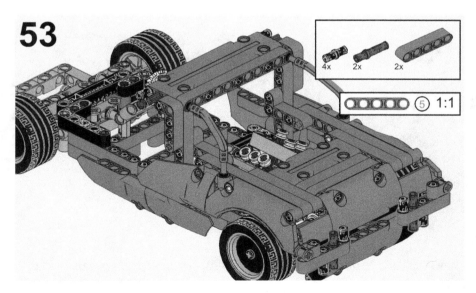

***Figure 3-22.*** *Put on the 5M beams with 3M and regular connector pegs*

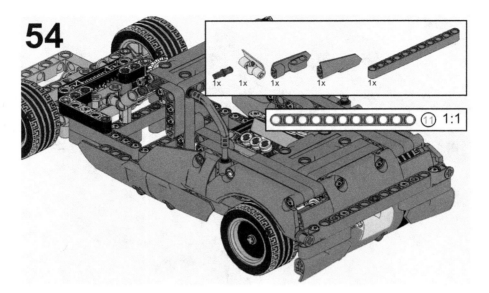

***Figure 3-23.*** *Put on the 11M beam, with the #21 and #22 panel fairings. Then put on the connector peg/cross axle and the panel curved 2 × 3 × 1*

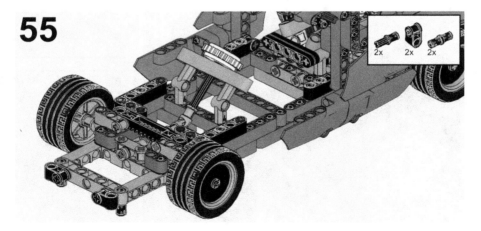

***Figure 3-24.*** *Put on the connector pegs, connector peg/cross axles, and the 90-degree cross blocks*

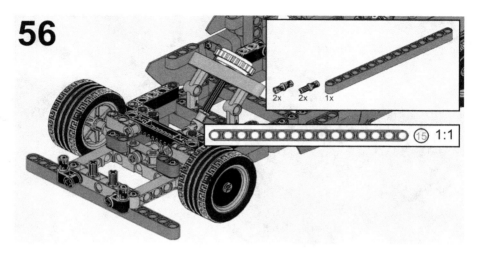

*Figure 3-25.* *Put on the 15M beam with the connector pegs and connector peg/cross axles*

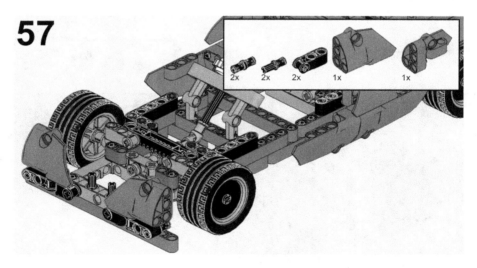

*Figure 3-26.* *Put on the panel fairing #1 and #2, and then put on the connector peg/cross axles, 3M cross blocks with axle, and then the connector pegs*

91

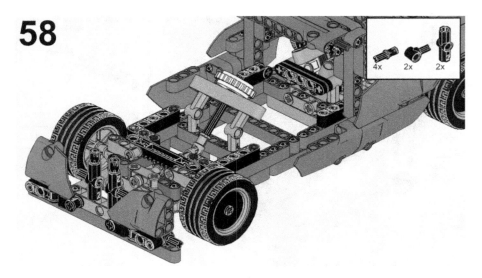

*Figure 3-27.* Put on the angle connector #2, the connector peg/cross axles, and the axle and pin connector hub with one axle

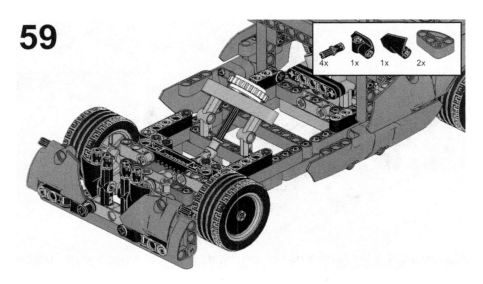

*Figure 3-28.* Put on the L-shaped quarter ellipse thick 2 × 3, the #7 and #8 panel fairings, and the connector peg/cross axles

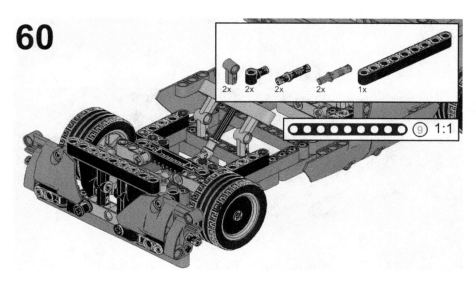

**Figure 3-29.** *Put on the axles 1M with pin 2M, the 3M connector pegs, the pins with pin holes, the #1 angle connectors, and 7M beam*

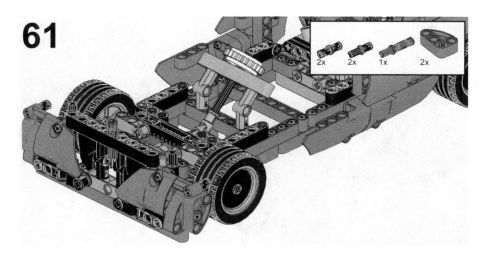

**Figure 3-30.** *Put on the 1M axle and 2M pin, then the connector pegs, the connector peg/cross axles, and the L-shape quarter ellipse 2 × 3*

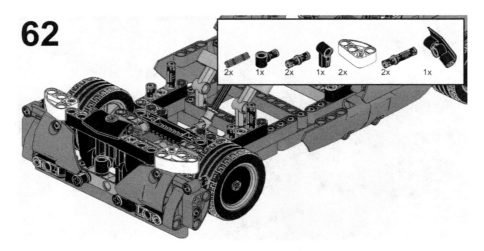

**62**

*Figure 3-31.* *Use the panel curved #3 2 × 3 × 1 angled, L-shape quarter ellipse 2 × 3, 2M axles, the connector pegs (both types), and the #1 angle connector with pin with pin hole*

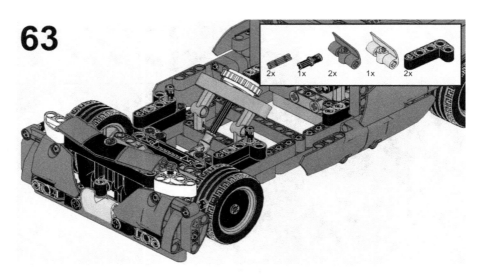

**63**

*Figure 3-32.* *Put on the 2 × 4 beams, panel curved 2 × 3 × 1, 2M axles, and the connector peg/cross axles*

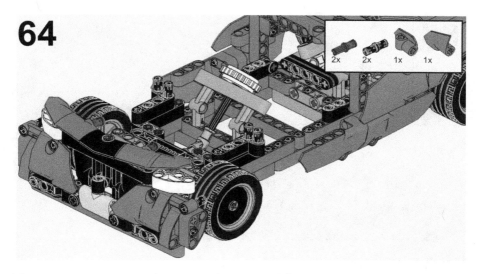

***Figure 3-33.*** *Put on the #7 and #8 panel fairings, the connector pegs, and the connector peg/cross axles*

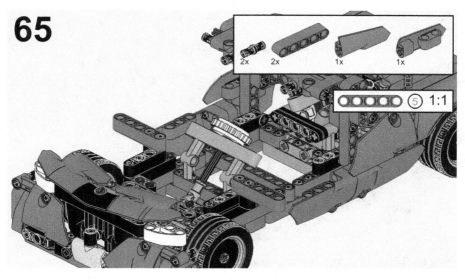

***Figure 3-34.*** *Use the #21 and #22 panel fairings, the 5M beams, and the connector pegs*

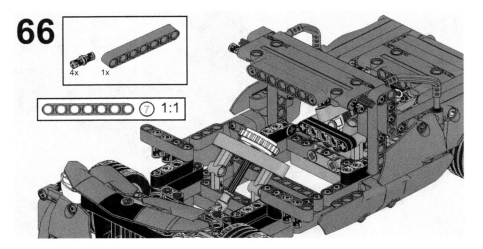

***Figure 3-35.*** *Put on the 7M beam and then the connector pegs*

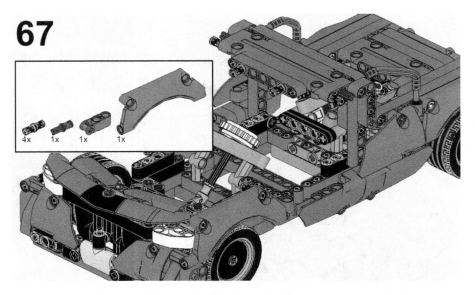

***Figure 3-36.*** *Put on the mudguard arched #30 9 × 2 × 3, 3M cross block with axle hole, connector peg/cross axle, and connector pegs*

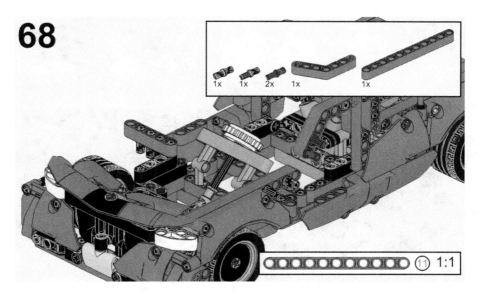

**Figure 3-37.** *Put in the 11M beam, the connector pegs, the connector peg/cross axles, and the 4 × 4 bent beam*

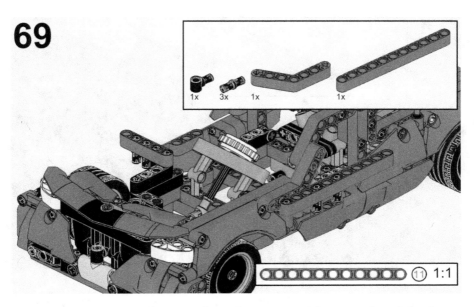

**Figure 3-38.** *Put on the 4 × 4 bent beam, 11M beam, pin with pin hole, and connector pegs*

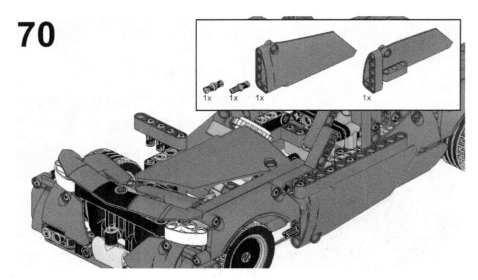

*Figure 3-39.* *Put on the #17 and #18 panel fairings, and put on the connector peg and connector peg/cross axle*

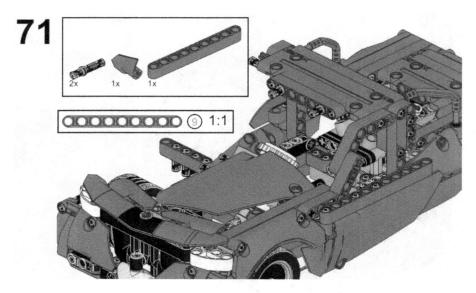

*Figure 3-40.* *Put on the 9M beam, 3M connector pegs, and panel fairing #8*

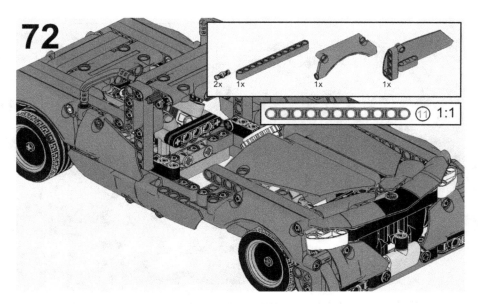

***Figure 3-41.*** *Use the 11M beam, connector pegs, the mudguard arched #30 9 × 2 × 3, and the panel fairing #18*

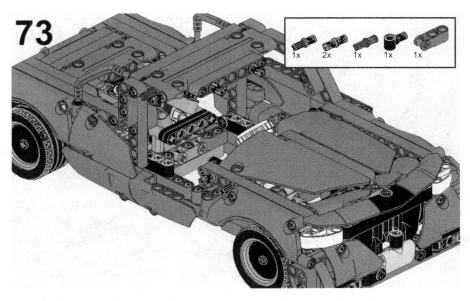

***Figure 3-42.*** *Put on the connector pegs, connector peg/cross axles, pin with pin hole, and 3M cross block with axle hole*

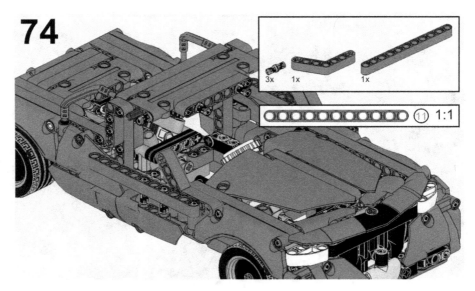

*Figure 3-43.* *Use the 11M beam, the connector pegs, and the 4 × 4 bent beam*

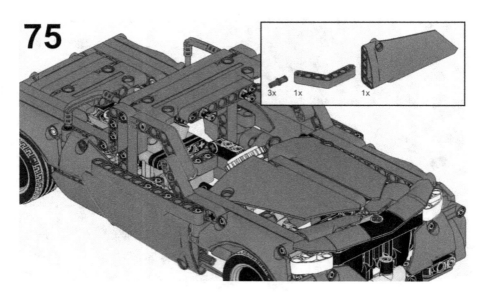

*Figure 3-44.* *Put on the connector peg/cross axles, the 4 × 4 bent beam, and the panel fairing #17*

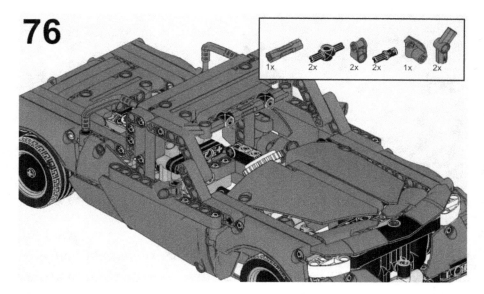

**Figure 3-45.** *Put on the 3M axle connector, the axle and pin connector with two axles, cross blocks, connector peg/cross axles, and #4 angle connectors*

# So, What Does It All Mean?

This is one of those times where I had to look at the original model versus what I ended up with, or at least what Stud.io shows in its Render function.

***Figure 3-46.*** *A comparison of the Dodge Charger SXT with LEGO Technic model*

I'm going to be honest and say that I could have done better, but it definitely is better than my first version of this. However, if you compare any LEGO Technic car model to its actual car, you will find similar types of differences.

Let's start with the positives. I do have a hood that I can open and close, not to mention a trunk. The side doors on the left and right can open and shut realistically as well.

As for the rest, you will find that you need to work with what you are given, but real cars are not made to look like LEGO. It is fortunate that you can manipulate some of these wing-like LEGO panels to match the curves of a car like the Dodge Charger SXT, but it isn't always a one-to-one spot-on match.

For example, the front part of the car was so full of curves, and I did my best to match it as best as I could. Try as I might, I never could get how the front bumper curves into the fender, bringing a custom-made headlight into its shape. I did my best to match it, leaving awkward gaps in the construction that I'm hoping the viewer just kinds of tunes out.

Sort of like how all LEGO Technic cars don't really have glass. The best that most builders do is create a shape around what the windshield would look like. Since most cars are very curvaceous with the front and back glass, the best thing you can do is imitate the curves with angle elements and flexible hose pieces, like what I did here.

The biggest challenge that you will run into is how it will all come together, which is also the most fun that you will ever have. When it came to the mudguard pieces, I knew I wanted them there, but I had to create some kind of framework for that and to make certain that framework integrated with the foundation laid in Chapter 2.

Even though the instructions showed a different type of steps, I started with the front, attempting to match the bumper as best as I could. Then I did the same for the back and then tried to join them together, making certain that the left and right sides of the car matched. I realize that this is a very generic building advice, so I recommend just getting out the bricks and getting started on whatever car that you want to build. In fact, I will also recommend creating a different base than the one that I provided here, because you might want to do other types of functions.

# Conclusion

The biggest problem with building something in LEGO Technic is making it look as much like the actual vehicle that you are modeling. Fortunately, LEGO offers many pieces that can construct the basic shape of what you are looking for.

However, just getting the basic shape is difficult, when you need to build upon what you have there with the placement of the wheels and all of the features. Fortunately, there are ways to do it, and there are many pieces that allow you to do just such a thing. The importance is to keep trying to imitate the shapes as best as you can with buildings and rebuildings, until you have something that you are satisfied with.

However, since the build is done, more can be done from there, including putting a motor on it, something discussed in the next chapter.

# CHAPTER 4

# Introducing the LEGO Motors and Remotes

In the last two chapters, I showed you how to make a Technic car, with the emphasis in Chapter 2 about the steering and realistic engine, while Chapter 3 focused on the actual shell of the car. If you apply the lessons from that, you can make any car in LEGO Technic, even if it will take a few drafts to get it looking the way that you want it.

However, wouldn't it be great if you had something that you could take control, as in remote control? That is what I intend to cover here. Now, you could be in a situation where you have a car and are just pushing it around the floor, but this is how to really bring it to life. And by bringing it to life, it will be zooming on the ground, going in whatever direction that you want it to go from a good distance.

## Introducing the LEGO Motors and Remotes

I suppose that I could have covered the Power Functions while talking about pieces in Chapter 1, but there is a lot to talk about when it comes to these motorized pieces, as there are a lot that you can do with these.

Now, before I go on, I want to say that these are not the only remotes, motors, and other such electric pieces that can be used with LEGO or LEGO Technic. Fans of the LEGO MINDSTORMS will notice that all of the

© Mark Rollins 2024
M. Rollins, *The Ultimate LEGO Technic Book*, Maker Innovations Series,
https://doi.org/10.1007/979-8-8688-0793-0_4

pieces are missing, and I go into greater detail in my book about LEGO MINDSTORMS EV3, but not any of the older versions.

Also, you may discover that you are not able to go to the LEGO website and order these Power Functions. There are similar ones there, and yes, you will need to adjust the main model below if you want to work with them. That, or you could go to BrickLink or similar LEGO shopping site and purchase these motors.

As I have said before, the one who decides your builds isn't me, it is you. If you want to make it different, or can make it better, then you should. This book is meant to be a framework of what you can do with LEGO Technic, not the actual painting within the frame, which is going to be your handiwork.

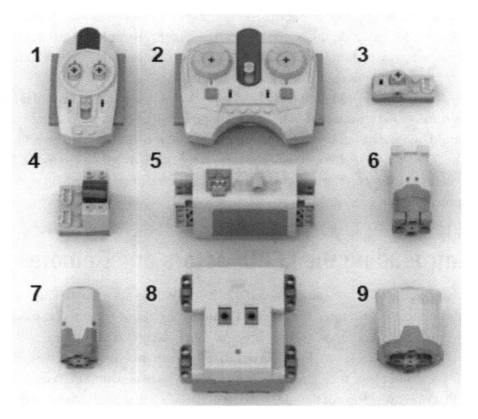

***Figure 4-1.***  *Various LEGO Power Functions*

So, let's look at what we have:

1) Electric Power Functions 9V Remote Control Unit (58122c01)

    This is just one of the remote controls, and it operates using three AAA batteries. There are two levers, one with a red designation on the left and one with blue on the right. There is also a switch with four locking positions, which will determine what device it will sync up with.

2) Electric Power Functions IR Speed Remote Control (64227c01)

    This is very similar to the 9V Remote Control Unit and also requires three AAA batteries to operate. Instead of levers that go forward and backward, it has two twistable sections. The red buttons are made to be a full stop, and it works rather well. It also has a switch section in the middle made for what device to sync it to.

3) Electric Pole Reverser (bb0339c01)

    This is essentially a part that will allow you to reverse the direction of motion on a motor, or put it in the center to stop it.

4) Electric Power Functions Receiver Unit (58123c01)

    This is a part which will allow you to hook up more than one motor or other device, and then you can sync it with one of the remote controls. Considering that a lot of models require more than one power function, this will come in handy for a lot of things. There is a sync switch on the other side which is made to sync with a remote.

5)  Electric 9V Battery Box 4 × 11 × 7 (59510c01)

    If you are going to use a motor or anything, then
    you will need a power source. This 9V battery
    box, which requires six AA batteries, is that power
    source. You can see the switch on top which
    designates the direction, and there is a pad that uses
    traditional LEGO studs for a secure LEGO electronic
    connection.

6)  Electric Motor 9V Power Functions (99499c01)

    This is just one motor (LEGO makes many), but one
    that I use as primary power, as this thing can really
    pack a punch.

7)  Electric Motor 9V Power Functions (58120c01)

    Another motor, with this having a base that can affix
    to traditional LEGO studs.

8)  Electric 9V battery box powered up two switches
    (bb1165c01)

    This type of battery box can power two motors,
    one at a time or simultaneously. It requires six AA
    batteries to operate and takes up a lot of space.

9)  Electric Motor 9V Power Functions XL (58121c01)

    This motor is wider than the other 9V motors.

# The LEGO Steering

I have to admit, when I first start making these things, I followed the model
of the steering system that I used in Chapter 2, only put a motor to link
with the rack and pinion. The issue that I had with that was the motor

would spin the gear too fast, and you would hear this ack...which would throw a lot of things off.

Basically, the challenge is to get it to turn slower, and at first, I thought the solution was to switch out the gear with a bigger gear. That did help, but it would often still get jammed up.

The solution was to use a worm gear which turned very slowly, but it used a mechanism. This really worked out well.

# The LEGO Motor

Of course, there is no point in steering a vehicle if it won't go. Fortunately, I'm going to give it some rear-wheel drive. Don't worry, we'll discuss four-wheel drive and even steering in the next chapter.

This involves using a differential to spin the back wheels, and it is going to be very strong. I did the directions a little differently than in the last two chapters, as I wanted to give an explanation on why the steps are done. Hopefully, this will help you learn how to create future LEGO Technic projects.

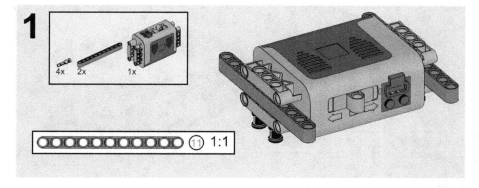

***Figure 4-2.*** *This is where you use the battery pack and then use the 11M beams with the friction snaps to hold them in place*

Since you will need a battery pack to power this creation, you might as well use it as base, and everything is going to be built out from it.

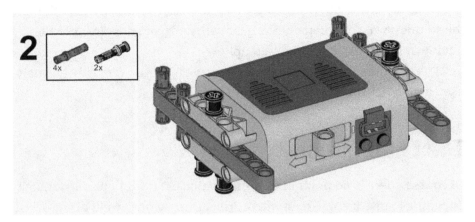

*Figure 4-3.* *Insert the 3M connector pegs as shown, as well as the friction snap to secure it in place*

At this point, you will be concentrating building on one side of the creation for the steering, so the base needs to be secured in place.

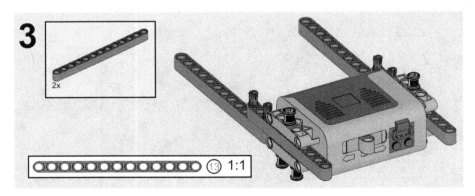

*Figure 4-4.* *This is where you add on the 15M beams, underneath the other beams*

The beams are made to add onto the structure and begin the steering.

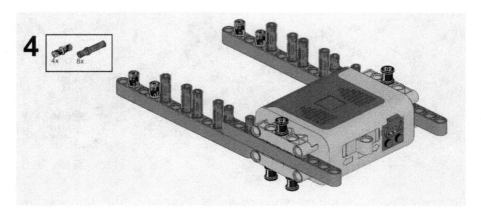

***Figure 4-5.*** *In this step, it is time to add the connector pegs, both the 2M and 3M type, as shown*

This is a lot of planting connector pegs, but this will help really strengthen the form here.

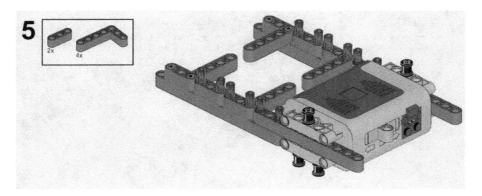

***Figure 4-6.*** *This is where you add the beams, both the 3M beams and the four 3 × 5 beams*

This is where you put in some beams that will secure a motor later.

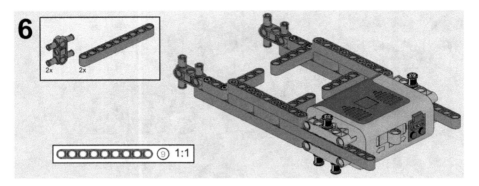

***Figure 4-7.*** *This is where you add the H-Shaped connector pegs, and the beams are there to hold it together*

What we are going to see here is how the beams really secure the other beams in place.

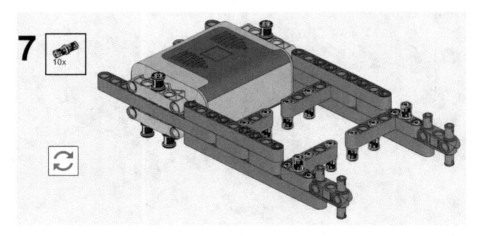

***Figure 4-8.*** *After you flip over the model, this is where you can add the connector pegs*

The connector pegs are here to hold some things in place later.

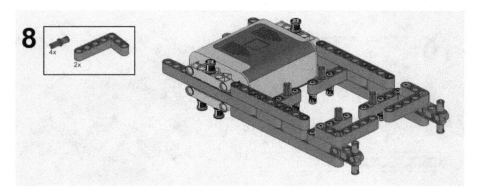

*Figure 4-9.* *This is where you add the 3 × 5 beams and also add the four connector peg with axles*

The 3 × 5 beams are meant to hold the cross blocks in place, and the connector peg with axles is going to hold a motor made for steering in place.

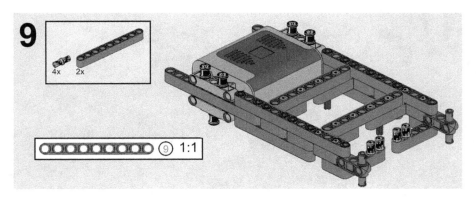

*Figure 4-10.* *Go ahead and add the 9M beams, which will really hold it together, and make certain to add the four connector pegs*

The 9M beams are made to hold the 3 × 5 beams into place, and there is a lot to do with the connector pegs much later.

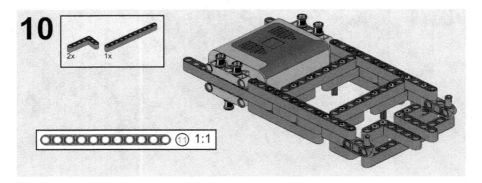

***Figure 4-11.*** *There is one 11M beam added here, as well as the two 3 × 5 beams*

The 3 × 5 beams are to set up for the steering later, and the 11M beam is made to sway for the steering.

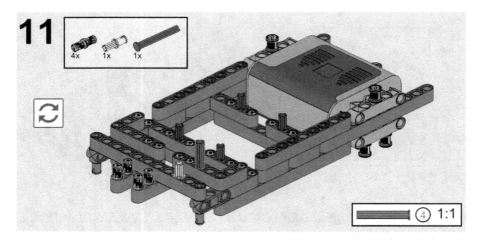

***Figure 4-12.*** *Insert the four connector pegs and the connector peg with axle (and without friction) as shown*

When you insert the 4M axle with stop from the bottom, it will not stay there on its own, but it will. The connector peg with axle is off-center, but it is there for a valid reason.

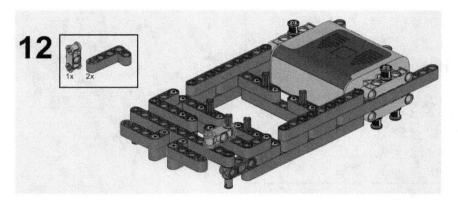

***Figure 4-13.*** *By adding on the double cross block, this will hold the axle with stop in place. The 2 × 4 beams can be placed into place*

The double cross block is placed there to really help with the steering, which will be permanently locked into place in later steps.

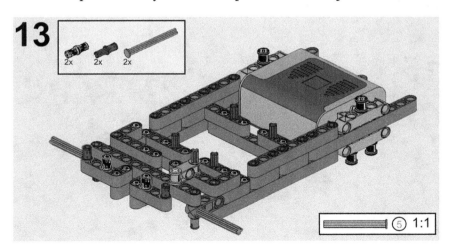

***Figure 4-14.*** *Add in the 5M axles with stops, and they will not stay in place for now. The connector pegs and the connector pegs with axles will snap into place*

In case you haven't figure this out, the 5M axles will hold the wheels on.

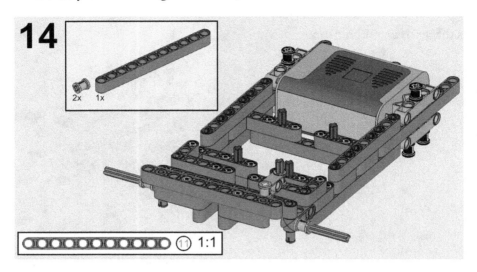

**Figure 4-15.** *Put on the 11M beam and slide on the bushes on each of the axles with stops to secure them in place*

The 11M beam is used to really secure the steering, and the bushes are going to help the wheels in their place.

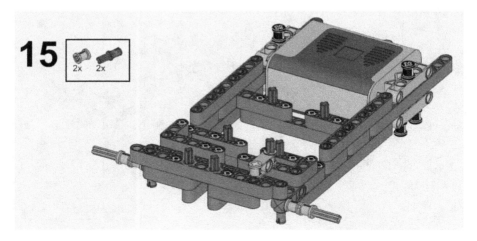

**Figure 4-16.** *Go ahead and put another bush on the axles with stops, and place the connector pegs with axles on the 11M beam from the last step*

The bushes are meant as another stop for the wheels, and the connector pegs with axles are another place to hold the steering.

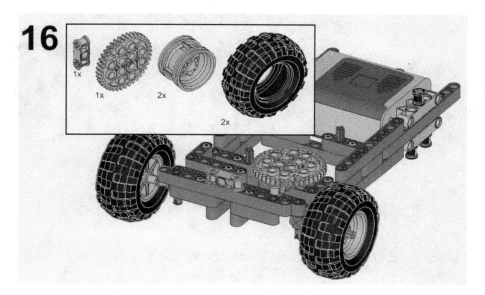

*Figure 4-17. Even though the back half of the vehicle is not done as yet, it would be a good time to slide on the wheels on the front*

So, the double cross block is going to hold something into place, and the 40-tooth gear is going to be used for steering.

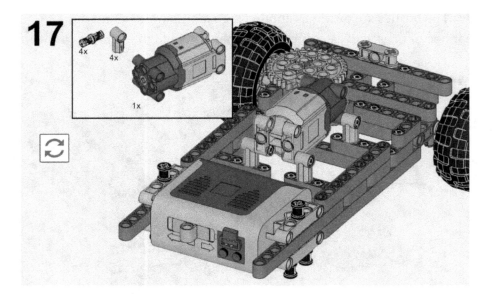

*Figure 4-18.* *Put in the motor on the angle elements #1*

In this step, you need to turn the model around so you can see the connector pegs with axles. You will need to take the motor and insert the connector pegs on the through holes on the bottom of it. Then snap in the #1 angle elements atop the connector pegs, and fit the entire construction on the main build as shown.

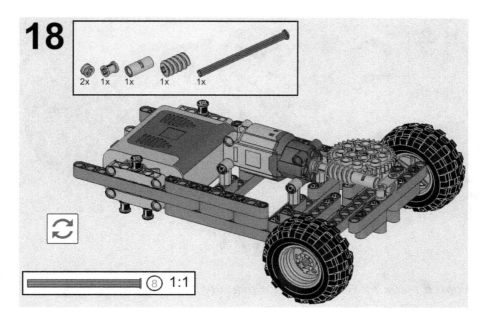

***Figure 4-19.*** *This is a step that includes putting these pieces on this 8M axle with stop in this order: half bush, bush, worm gear, 2M tube, and half bush*

You can tell that you do it right when the teeth of the 40-tooth gear meshes with the worm gear. The motor will then spin the worm gear, which will turn the 40-tooth gear, which will turn the front two wheels.

This will conclude the steering section part of this construction, and now it is time to focus on the motor section, what will make the car go.

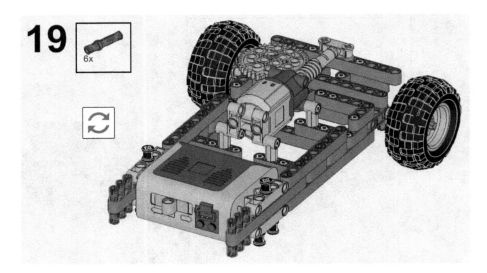

*Figure 4-20.* *The 3M connector pegs are centered on the end of the 11M beam as shown*

Time to shift focus and turn the model around, with a similar beginning like the steering column.

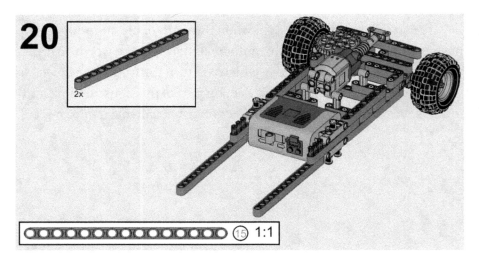

*Figure 4-21.* *Put on the 15M beam on the end of the 3M connector pegs*

This 15M beam is going to hold the other end of the wheels, and they are going to need a motor for spinning them.

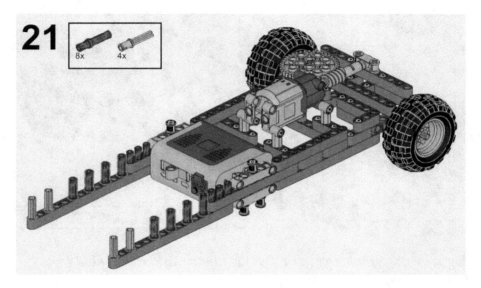

*Figure 4-22.* *Put on the four 3M connector pegs as shown, as well as the two connector peg with 2M axles*

Like the support of the other side, these connector pegs are made for holding more into place in later steps.

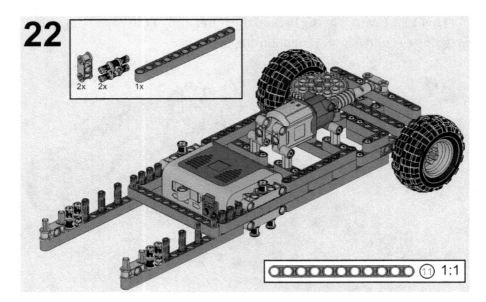

*Figure 4-23.* *Time to put on the 11M beam and the double cross blocks, along with the other two pieces*

It is going to be pretty obvious why the connector pegs are there in the next few steps, which are going to be off the model, which will be inserted later.

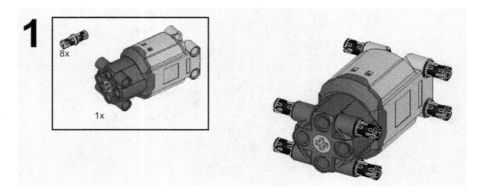

*Figure 4-24.* *Insert the connector pegs on the motor*

You might not be able to see this, but the connector pegs go in all through holes on both sides of the motor.

**Figure 4-25.** *Insert the T-beams on the connector pegs, and insert the 90-degree cross blocks as shown*

This going to be a time to put in the beams and the cross blocks to make this work.

**Figure 4-26.** *The connector pegs are put on the T-beams, and the 3M axles go as follows*

The connector pegs will hold on more, and the 3M axles will not stay in this position for later.

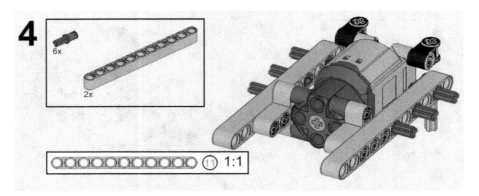

**Figure 4-27.** *Time to put on the 11M beam and the connector peg with axles*

All you need to do is just put on the connector peg with axles for later, once again.

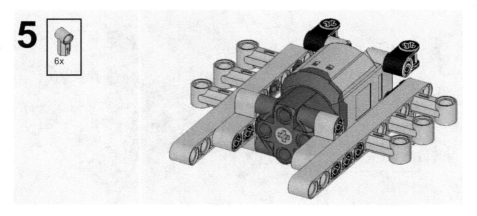

**Figure 4-28.** *Insert the #1 angle connectors on the connector peg axles*

Put on the #1 angle connectors, and now, it is time to insert this onto the main construction.

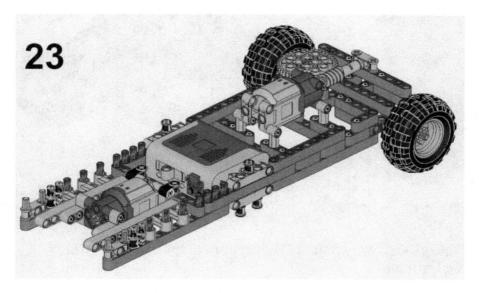

*Figure 4-29.* *Put on the motor from the last few steps, and the secure them with the 3M axles*

This is going to be one of those times where you insert all the motor on the 3M connector pegs, and it will click into place.

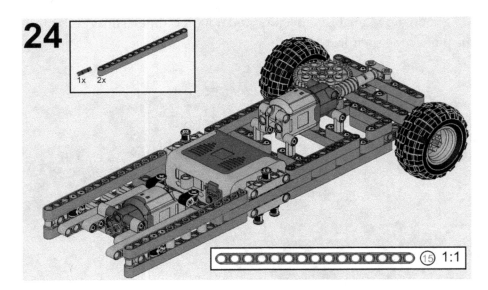

**Figure 4-30.**  *Put on the 15M beams, with the 2M axle on the electric motor*

This is really going to hold the motor and everything else on.

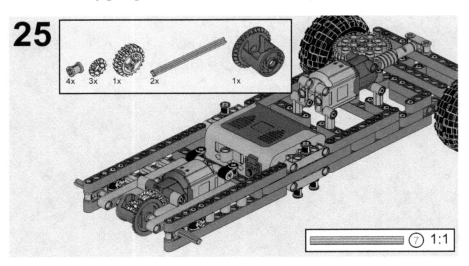

**Figure 4-31.**  *Put on the gear first, and then put on the differential with three gears on it. Put on the 11M axle with the bushes*

This will really link the wheel axle to the motor.

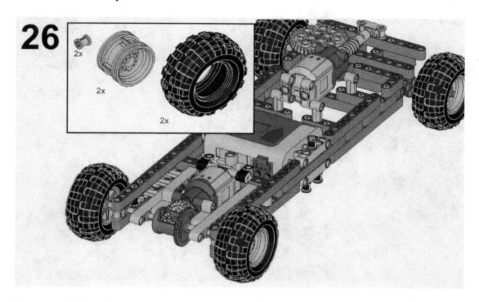

*Figure 4-32.* *Time to put on the wheels*

Now that the wheels are put on, it is still not finished, as you need to make it run.

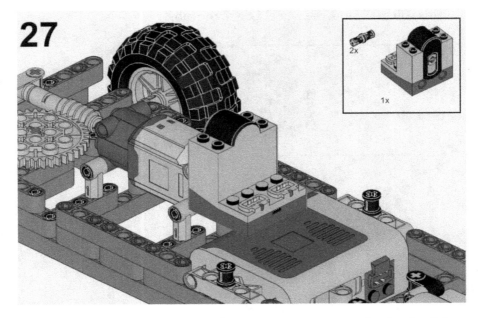

***Figure 4-33.*** *Once you put on the connector pegs on the back of the motor, install the Electric Power Functions Receiver Unit*

Now, once you have this the Electric Power Functions Receiver Unit, you will need to connect that to the 9V battery box. There is a wire that affixes to the port with two studs and that metallic tabs. All you need to do is turn on the battery power switch, and there will be a green light indicator.

I recommend connecting the wire from the motor in the front for steering to the red port on the Receiver Unit and then connecting the wire that propels the rear wheels to the Receiver Unit's blue port. Then what you will need to do is make certain that the remote that you use is synced with the Electric Power Functions Receiver Unit, and you will now have control of steering on the left with acceleration on the right.

You can have a lot of fun with this, but you also will want to make certain that you don't steer too far one way or the other, as this could jam things up. Similar hang-ups can happen to the back motor, so check on it from time to time while in use.

# Conclusion

What you see here was the instructions of how to create a LEGO car that can go forward and backward, not to mention steering to the left and right. This is one way to take control of a LEGO Technic car, as far as the steering and propulsion is concerned.

There are of course many other ways to do steering, but it really all comes down to creating a steering system that does not jam up while in motion. Jammed up steering can lead to damaged LEGO motors, and they can also cause individual LEGO pieces to break over time.

You also want to create propulsion systems that will not jam up as well, and pieces like a differential can create systems with reduced friction, so all that motion will be used on the road.

Whatever the case, you should be able to take control of it in order to allow your LEGO creation to go across the floor, or even outdoors with ease. However, is it possible to improve upon remote control by going with four-wheel drive and steering? The answer is absolutely!

# CHAPTER 5

# Problems That Arise with Four-Wheel Steering and Four-Wheel Drive

Now that we have covered how to make a car that can steer and go across the floor, it would be good to really kick it up a notch. Of course, you might be wondering what you can do after creating something that you can take control of, and that is a good question.

For starters, you can make the steering better, and you can make it so that the back wheels aren't the only thing that are turning. Yes, I am talking about creating a car that has four-wheel steering and four-wheel drive.

Hang on a second, you meant that it is possible to create a car with four-wheel steering as well as four-wheel drive? The answer to that is "yes," and I honestly don't think that LEGO has anything like this. Granted, LEGO has been around for decades, but my searches haven't revealed anything as yet. So, I'm just going to say that what I am giving you something unique, until LEGO makes it. I could be wrong by the time you read this.

© Mark Rollins 2024
M. Rollins, *The Ultimate LEGO Technic Book*, Maker Innovations Series,
https://doi.org/10.1007/979-8-8688-0793-0_5

# Four-Wheel Steering and Four-Wheel Drive

As I have said before, the purpose of this book isn't just to show you instructions and have you build them. When you finish this book, I want you not to think like a mechanic, but rather a creator.

When I wrote my first book about LEGO Technic, I wanted to include a section about a car with four-wheel drive and four-wheel steering. After a frustrating time, I decided against it and realized that I had to meet my deadline and simply excluded any section about a four-wheel drive car with four-wheel steering capacity. It still bothered me, and I eventually figured out a way to do it when I wrote LEGO Technic Robotics.

Creating a vehicle with four-wheel drive is not much of a problem. All you need to do is set up a motor so the two back wheels spin, as shown in Chapter 4 of this book. The method with the differential isn't the only way that can be done.

I believe that I have discussed the possibility of using two motors to create a very fun car that can make some awesome turns. All that is required is putting a motor on the left side and then putting the motor on the other side. Sync those up to a remote control, and you have a car that can make some pretty hard turns, and this method works very well for a tank with treads, something not really discussed in this book.

You could actually use four motors and get the same results, even hooking the remotes together and really having crazy fun. However, this is not how four-wheel drive cars work, because you can easily do the job with one engine. All that is required is simply connect all four wheels with axles so the tires will spin as one, backwards or forwards.

Granted, you might not need to have four-wheel drive on our Technic vehicles, but in the real world, a car with four-wheel drive can handle rough terrain. You will discover that your improved LEGO vehicle with four-wheel drive can handle some seriously deep carpet, even shag.

Linking axles and gears is something that is relatively simple, provided you know how. All you have to do is figure out a system of beams where the axles can be solid in their through holes and be certain that the gears have enough space to spin and be meshed together.

So yes, it is easy to make a network of Technic axles that mesh together underneath a vehicle and make the wheels spin. Well, it is actually a bit more complicated than that, but with a few designs, and some constant redesigns, the basic concept can be made into reality.

The problem that I kept having was how to steer this remotely. As early as Chapter 2, steering a vehicle is one of the most basic tenets in building a LEGO vehicle. It isn't difficult with a rack-and-pinion method, or even the worm-gear method demonstrated in the last chapter.

However, Chapter 4 demonstrated that the front two wheels have to swivel slightly in order to make steering possible. If these wheels are all connected to a mesh network of axles, how is this possible?

That was really where I had a difficult time, but I eventually figured out that with a certain part, this was possible. All that was required was a Technic universal joint, which allows a certain degree of flexibility.

Okay, so we're going to talk about how to make a car with four-wheel steering and four-wheel drive.

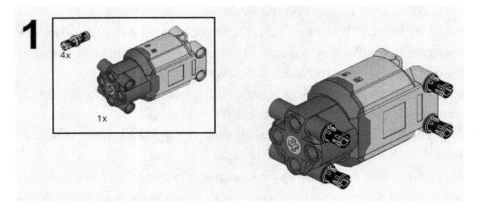

*Figure 5-1.* *Go ahead and put the connector pegs on the left side of the motor*

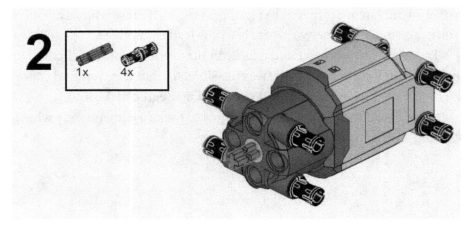

*Figure 5-2.* *The connector pegs can go on the other side of the motor, with a 2M axle in the middle*

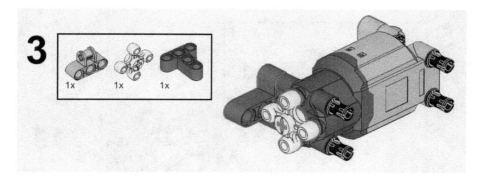

*Figure 5-3.* *Put the T-shaped beam on the side of the motor as shown and the 3M beam with cross axle on the other side. The gear in the middle goes right on the axle*

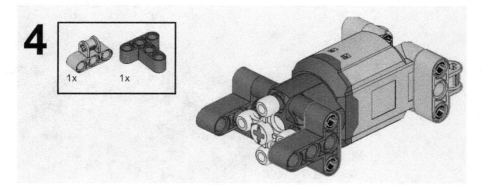

*Figure 5-4.* *Go ahead and put the 3M T-beam on the side with 3M beam with cross axle hole*

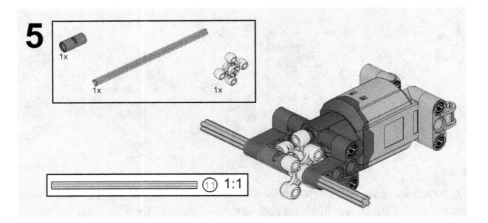

***Figure 5-5.*** *As you put the gear in with the 2M tube in between the two T-beams, use the 11M axle to keep those other two parts centered*

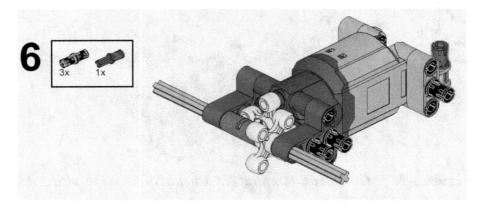

***Figure 5-6.*** *Put in the three connector pegs on one side and the connector peg with axle hole as shown*

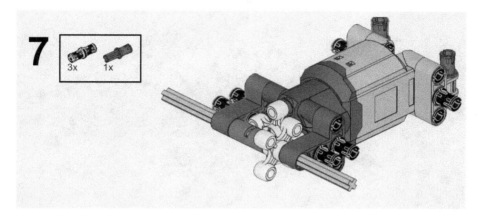

*Figure 5-7.* *Go ahead and put the connector pegs and the connector peg with axle on the other side as shown so they match the other side*

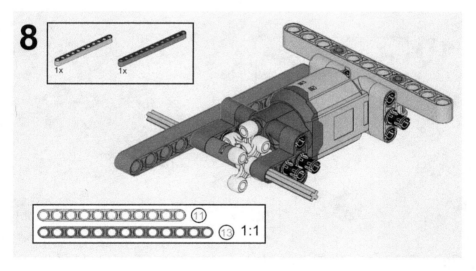

*Figure 5-8.* *The 13M beam goes on one side to lock into place, and the 11M beam goes to the back*

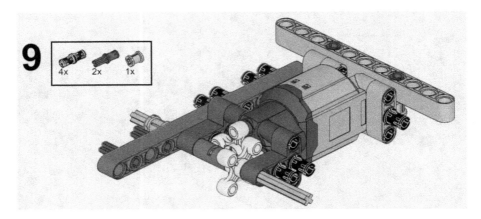

***Figure 5-9.*** *Put the connector pegs with axles on as shown, with the bush at the end of the 11M axle, so there is 1M of axle left for a future step. Don't forget the four connector pegs*

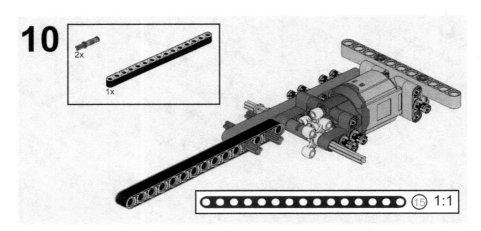

***Figure 5-10.*** *Use the 2M connector pegs with 1M axle to hold the 15M axle into place*

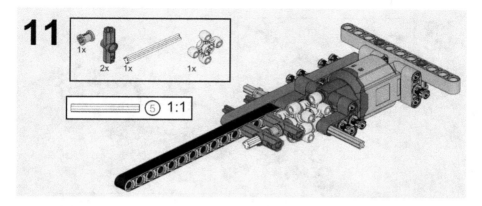

***Figure 5-11.*** *Insert the #2 angle connectors and then use the gear and the 5M axle and bush in the middle*

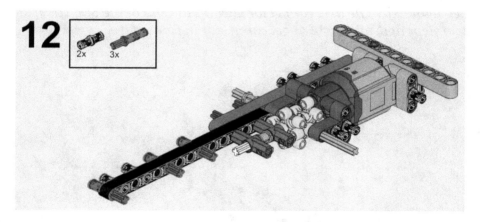

***Figure 5-12.*** *Insert the connector pegs with the 2M connector pegs with axles as shown*

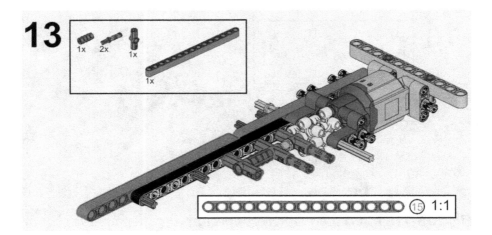

*Figure 5-13.* Attach the 15M beam on the end with the 2M connector peg with axle. The axle connector goes on the end of the 5M axle from two steps ago, with a #2 angel connector in front of it

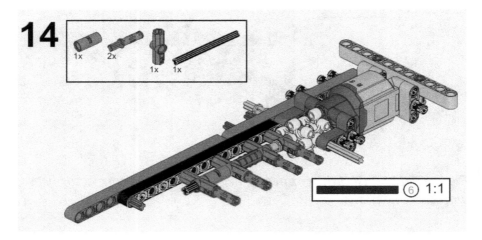

*Figure 5-14.* Time to put in the #2 angle connector and then put in the 6M axle with the 2M tube. You can then put on the 2M connector peg with axle

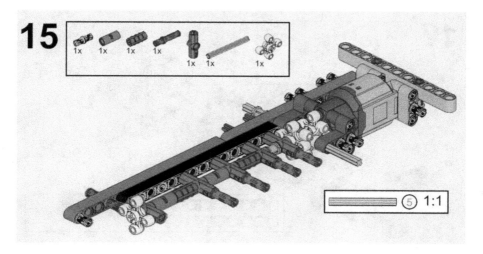

*Figure 5-15.* Use the 5M axle to connect the #2 angle connector, axle connector, 2M tube, and the gear. Put on the connector peg and the 3M connector peg as shown

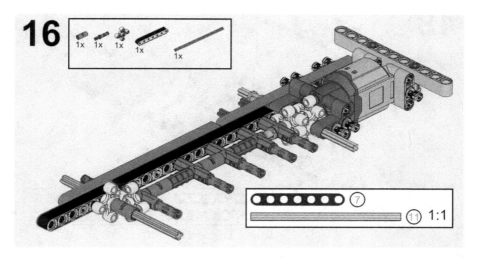

*Figure 5-16.* Connect the 7M beam and then insert the 11M axle with the tube and gear so it meshes

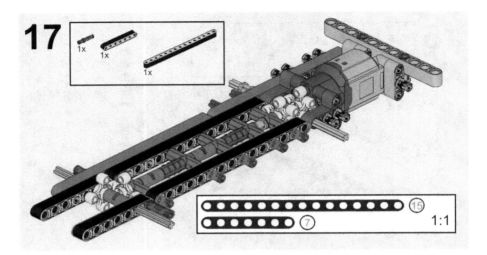

*Figure 5-17.* Time to snap on the 15M beam. Slide a 7M beam on the axle and insert the 3M connector peg

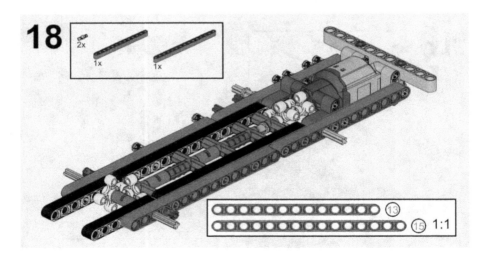

*Figure 5-18.* Time to snap on two beams with the 13M and 15M on the side, with the two connector pegs on the other side

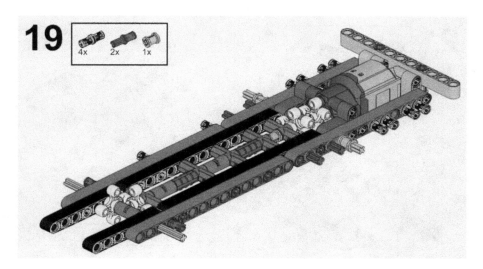

*Figure 5-19.* Go on and put the bush on with the connector pegs and the connector pegs with axles

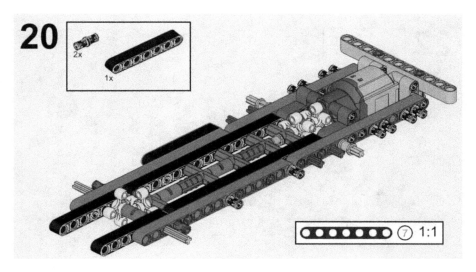

*Figure 5-20.* Go ahead and snap on a 7M beam on one side with the two connector pegs on the other

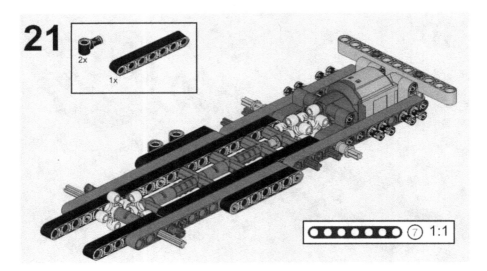

***Figure 5-21.*** *Put on the 7M beam on one side and the through holes with connector pegs on the other side as possible*

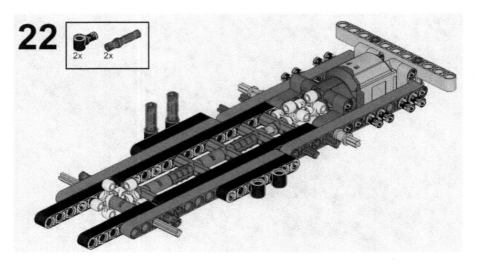

***Figure 5-22.*** *Insert the through holes with connector pegs on one side with the 3M connector pegs on the other*

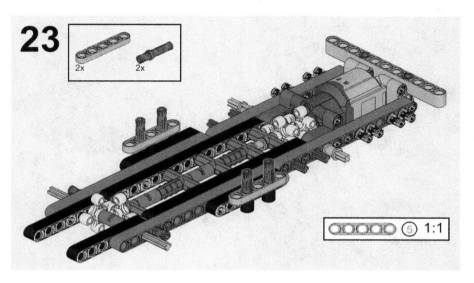

***Figure 5-23.*** *Go ahead snap on the 5M lever atop the 3M connector pegs from the last step, and then insert the 3M connector pegs on the other side with the 5M lever*

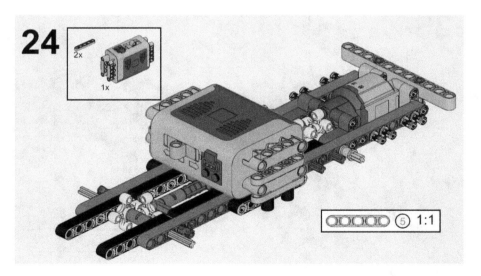

***Figure 5-24.*** *Slide the battery pack on the 3M connector pegs, and then slide the 5M levers on the 3M connector pegs as shown*

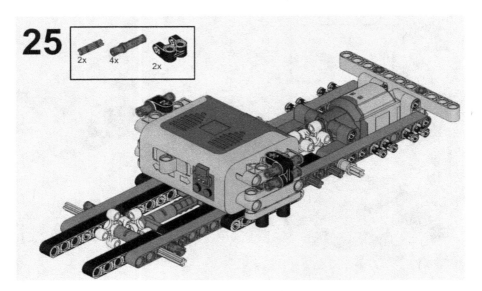

***Figure 5-25.*** *Insert the 2M connector blocks and use the 2M axles to secure them in place. Center the 3M connector pegs as shown*

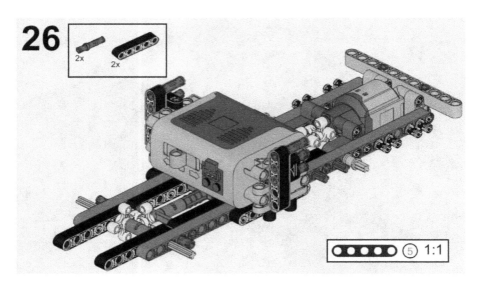

***Figure 5-26.*** *Snap on the 5M beam, and then put on the 3M connector pegs*

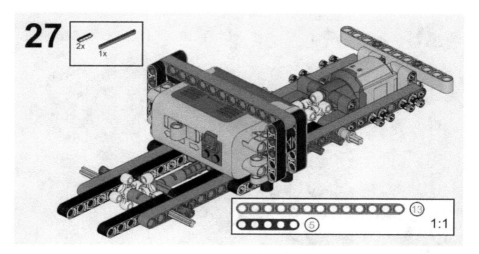

***Figure 5-27.*** *Put on the 13M beam on the 3M connector peg from the last step and the 5M beam on the other side of the other 5M beam*

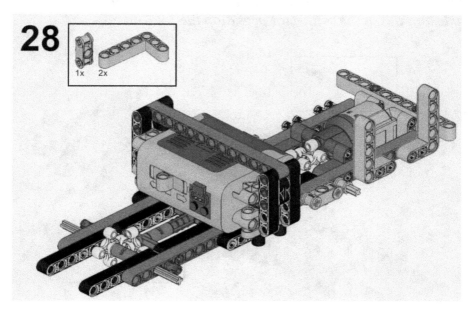

***Figure 5-28.*** *Slide on the cross blocks on the connector peg with cross axles, and then put on the 3 × 5 beams*

147

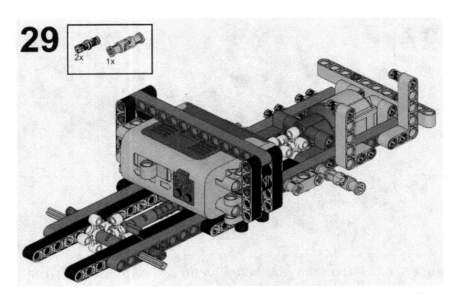

*Figure 5-29.* Time to put on the Technic universal joint on the 11M axle and put in the connector pegs atop the 3 × 5 beams

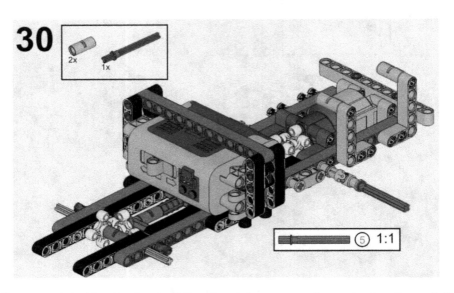

*Figure 5-30.* Put in the 5.5M axle with stop on the swivel axle and the 2M tubes on the connector pegs

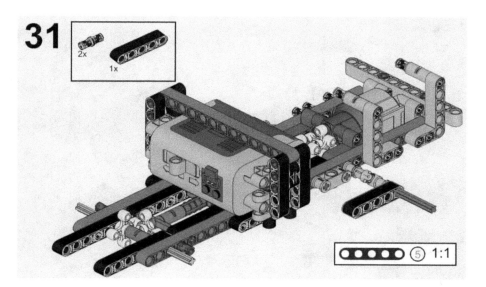

***Figure 5-31.*** *Slide on the 5M beam on the 5.5M axle, and then put on the connector pegs on the 2M tubes*

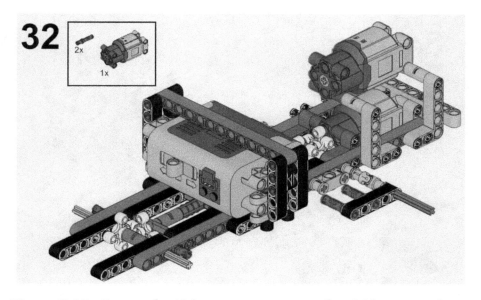

***Figure 5-32.*** *Put on the 3M connector pegs on the 5M beam, and then put the motor on the end of the 2M tubes*

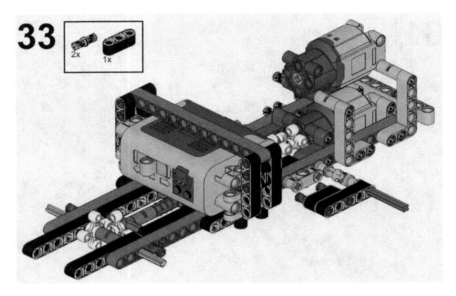

*Figure 5-33.* *Put the 3M beam on the 3M connector pegs, and put the connector pegs on the edge of the motor*

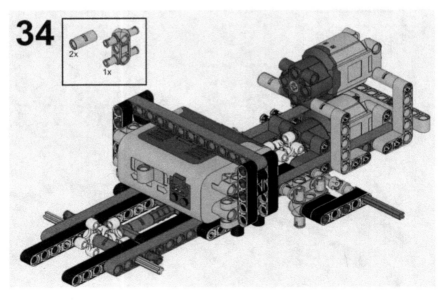

*Figure 5-34.* *Put the tubes on the opposite side of the motor as shown, and put on the H-shaped cross blocks there*

150

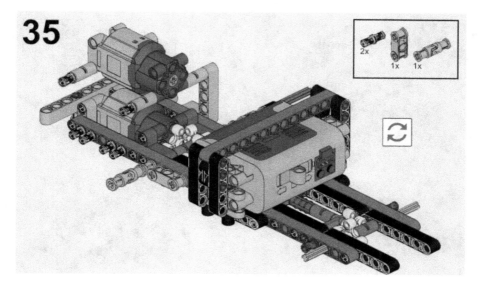

*Figure 5-35.* *Put in the connector pegs, the double cross block, and the flexible axle as shown*

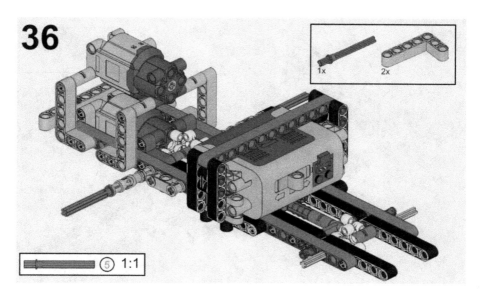

*Figure 5-36.* *Snap on the 3 × 5 beams to lock into place, and insert the 5.5M axles on the flexible axle connectors*

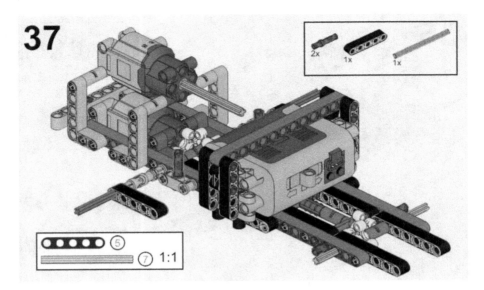

*Figure 5-37.* Insert the 3M connector pegs as shown, and then put on the 5M beams on the axles. Place the 7M axle on motor

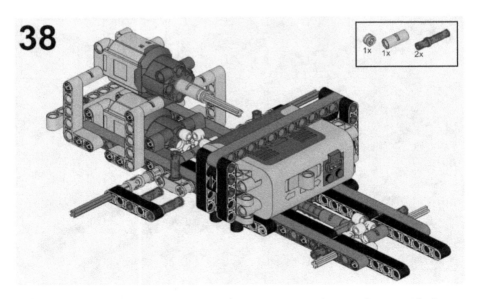

*Figure 5-38.* Insert the 3M connector pegs on the 5M beam. Slide on the tube and the half bush

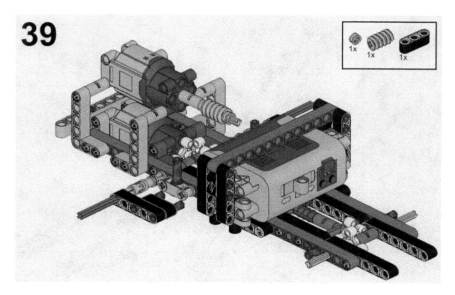

*Figure 5-39.* *Put the 3M beam on the 3M connector pegs from the last step, and slide on the worm gear and the half bush on the axle on the motor*

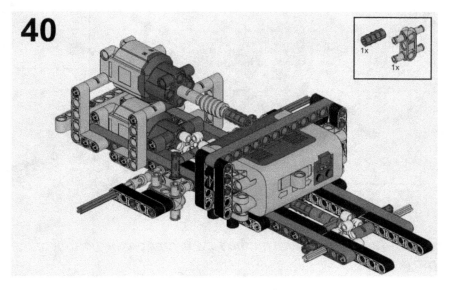

*Figure 5-40.* *Time to put on the H-shaped cross block and the axle connector*

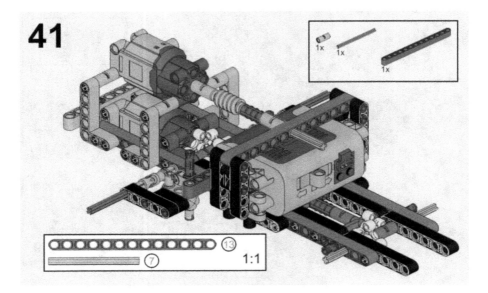

*Figure 5-41. Put on the 2M tube and the 7M axle and the 13M beam as shown*

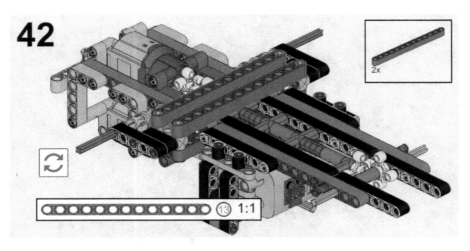

*Figure 5-42. Time to snap on the 13M beams on the bottom of the construction*

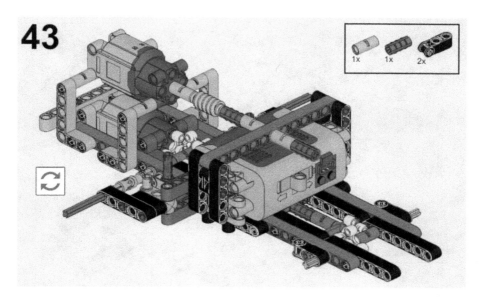

***Figure 5-43.*** *Put on the 2M tube and the axle connector and then 3M cross block with two through holes*

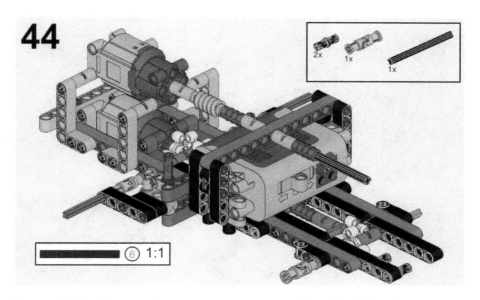

***Figure 5-44.*** *Put on the connector pegs and the flexible axle connector. Don't forget to put on the 6M axle*

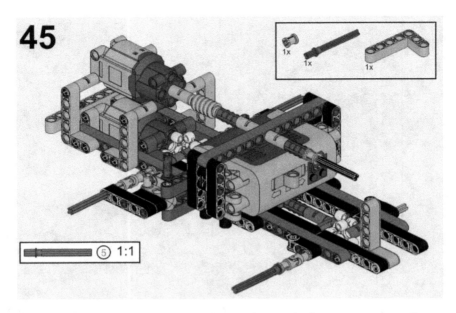

***Figure 5-45.*** *Insert the 5.5M axle, and attach the 3 × 5 Beam. Put on the bush on the axle*

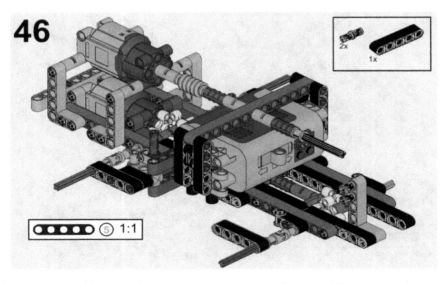

***Figure 5-46.*** *Put on the connector pegs on the 3 × 5 beam, and put on the 5M beam on the axle*

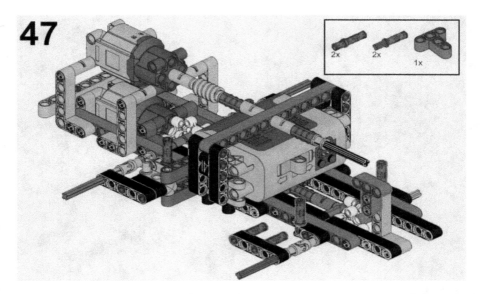

*Figure 5-47.* *Put on the T-beam, the 3M connector pegs, and the 2M connector pegs with axles*

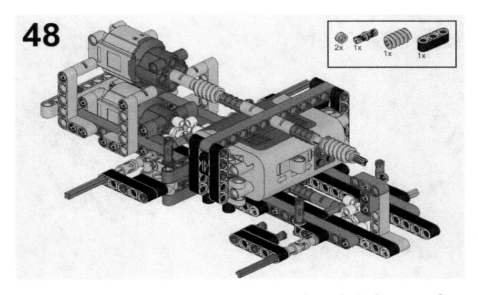

*Figure 5-48.* *Time to put on worm gear on the axle, in between the half bushes. Put on the 3M beam and the connector peg on top*

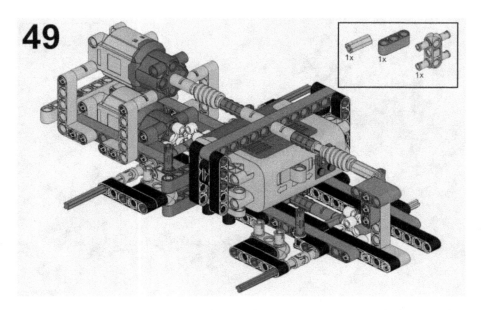

*Figure 5-49.* *Time to put on the 3M beam on top, with the axle connector on top. The H-shaped cross block goes on top*

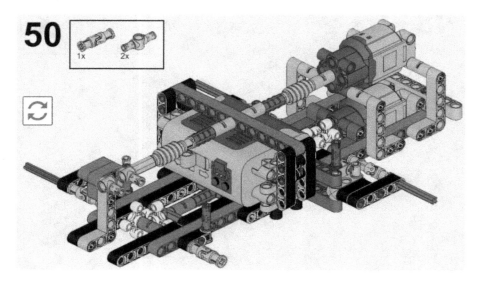

*Figure 5-50.* *Time to insert a flexible axle and then insert the 3M connector pegs with through holes*

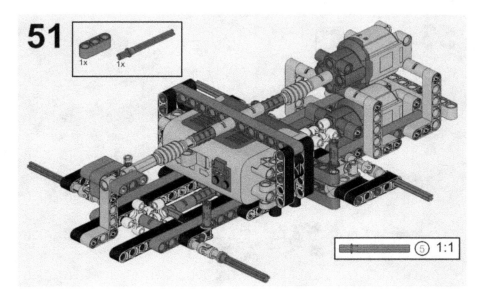

***Figure 5-51.*** *Put in the 3M beam and insert the 5.5M axle with stop*

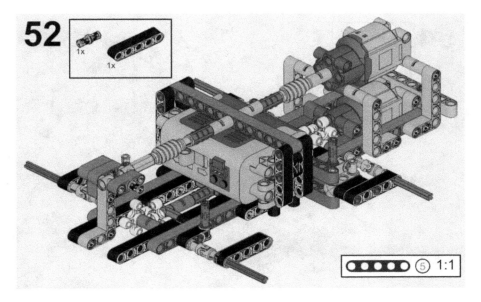

***Figure 5-52.*** *Insert the connector peg, and slide on the 5M beam on the axle from the last step*

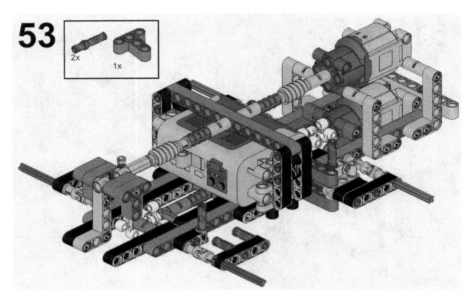

*Figure 5-53.* Add on the T-beam as well as the two 3M connector pegs

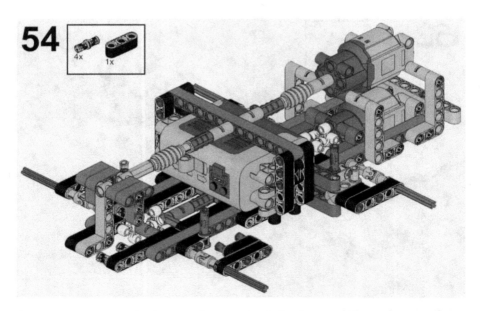

*Figure 5-54.* Put on the 3M beam, and the four connector pegs as shown

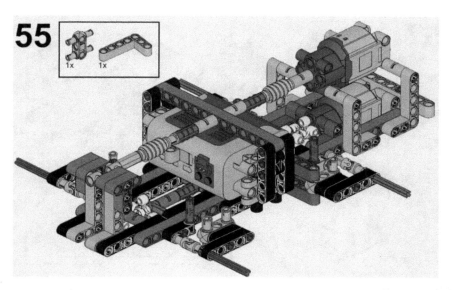

***Figure 5-55.*** *Time to put on the 3 × 5 beam, as well as the H-shaped cross block*

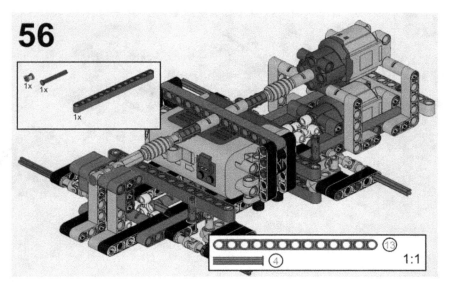

***Figure 5-56.*** *Use the 4M axle with stop to cap off the axle down the middle as shown. Then use the 13M beam*

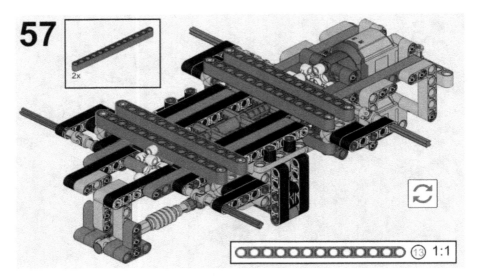

*Figure 5-57.* *Flip the model over and snap in the 13M beams, which will hold the front area into place*

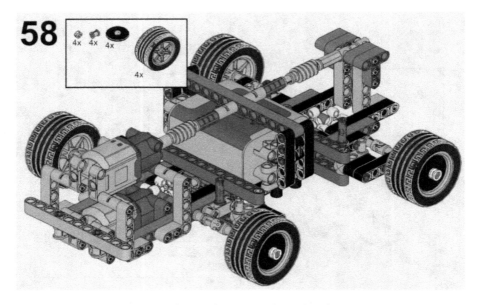

*Figure 5-58.* *This is where you put on the wheels*

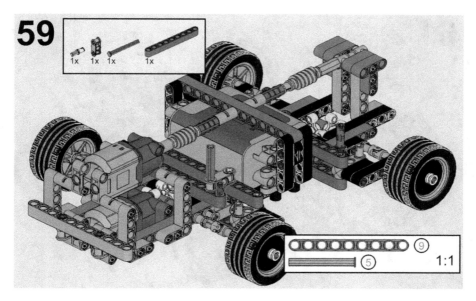

***Figure 5-59.*** *The next step is to put the 9M beam on, but first, put the 5M axle with stop through it. Put on the double cross block*

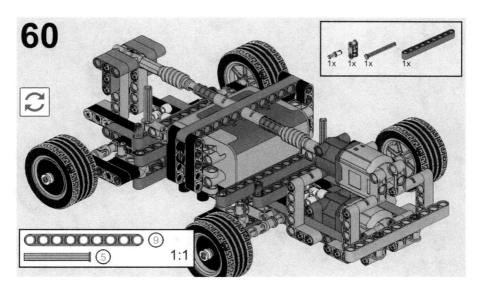

***Figure 5-60.*** *Time to repeat the last step on the other side*

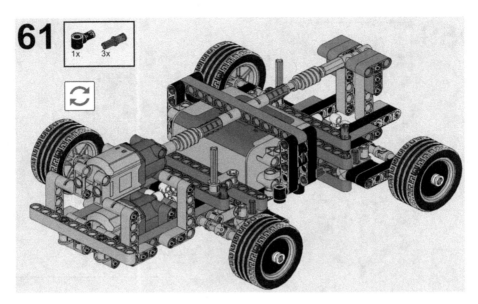

***Figure 5-61.*** *Time to put on the connector pegs with axles and the connector peg with through hole as shown*

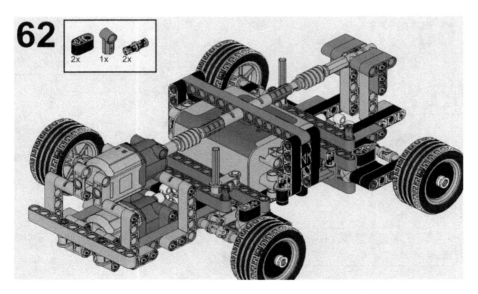

***Figure 5-62.*** *Time to put on the 2M beam with axle holes and a #1 angle connector with the connector pegs*

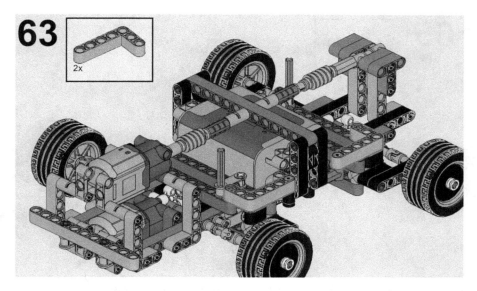

***Figure 5-63.*** *Time to snap on the 3 × 5 beams as shown*

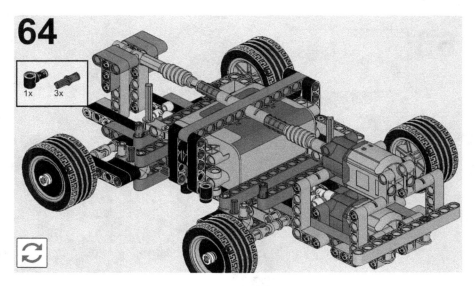

***Figure 5-64.*** *Time to put on the connector pegs with axles and the connector peg with through hole as shown*

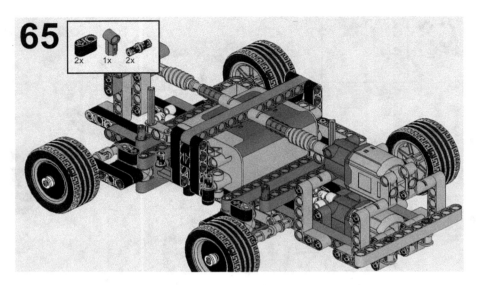

***Figure 5-65.*** *Time to put on the 2M beam with axle holes and a #1 angle connector with the connector pegs*

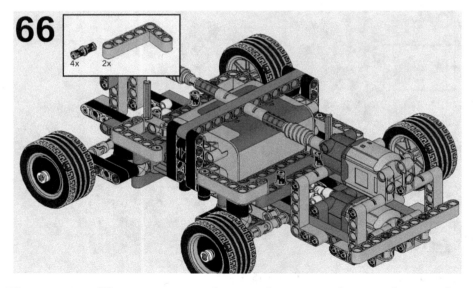

***Figure 5-66.*** *Time to snap on the 3 × 5 beams as shown, along with the four connector pegs*

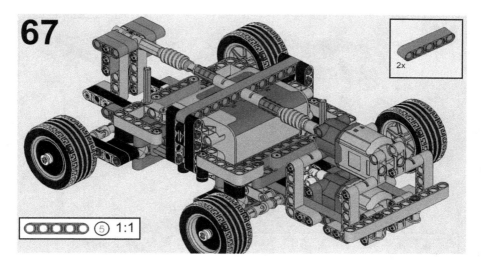

***Figure 5-67.*** *Time to put on the 5M beams*

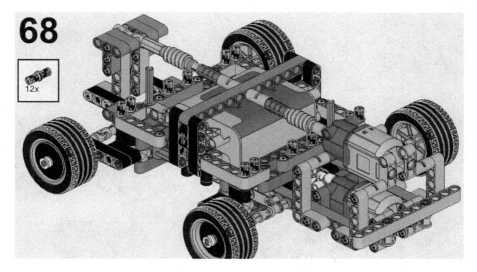

***Figure 5-68.*** *This is where you put on the twelve connector pegs*

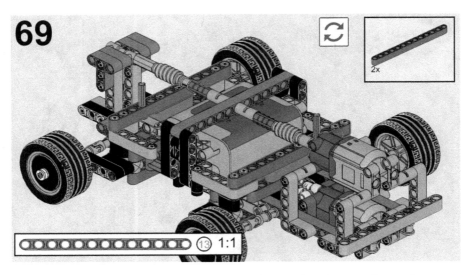

**Figure 5-69.** *Time to put on the 13M beam, but you will need to remove the 40-tooth gears before you do that*

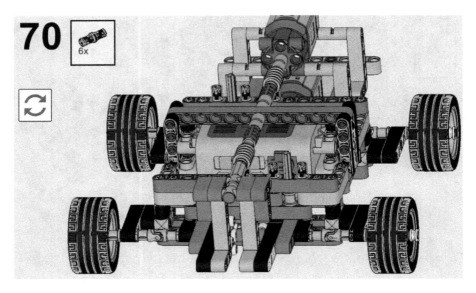

**Figure 5-70.** *Time to put on the six connector pegs*

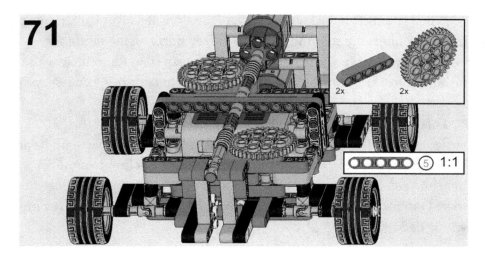

*Figure 5-71.* Time to add on the 5M beams and put the 40-tooth gears on

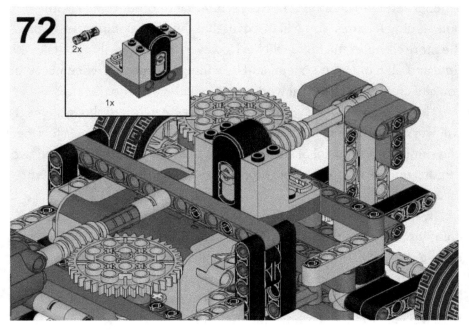

*Figure 5-72.* Insert the Electric Power Functions Receiver Unit on the top with two connector pegs

When you put on the Electric Power Functions Receiver Unit, I suggest that you connect the steering motor to the red port and the motor for propulsion to the blue port. This is just so you can steer the vehicle with the left control and control its speed with the right control. Of course, you can switch the controls if you like.

I had to admit that I was really challenged when I created this particular model, and I was really hoping that I could improve upon it with some shock absorbers. However, I could not figure out how to connect them and still have the functionality of four-wheel steering and four-wheel drive. Perhaps you can figure that out, but as for me, I had to finish by my writing deadline.

# Conclusion

When it comes to creating a LEGO Technic car or other vehicle with outstanding features, you will discover that the more complex you want, the more complex the build will be. However, if you are willing to take the time and plan out your system, and be willing to change it when necessary, you can create a system that works very well and does not jam up.

This is the case when you are trying to create two complex systems that will work together, like the four-wheel drive also has four-wheel steering. If you want to take control of such a system, then you are going to need two motors, one for the four-wheel propulsion and another to steer the four wheels of the car.

By far, the most complex is the steering mechanism, requiring a complex mechanism for each wheel that is still connected to a propulsion engine so the wheel can spin freely and still move so it can steer.

Figuring out how to do these types of systems is a fun and interesting challenge for any builder, and I am hoping that the instructions detailed here will lead to a lot of innovation for future LEGO Technic builders, pushing the edge as far as what a remote-controlled creation can do.

# CHAPTER 6

# LEGO Technic Helicopter

While helicopters are a fairly recent invention, they were first conceived centuries before their actual invention. As early as 400 BC, children of China were playing with bamboo flying toys with spinning rotors attached to a stick. All it takes a little bit of spinning, and lift is created, lifting the stick impressively, but only temporarily, in the air.

Some early designs of machines that would eventually lead to the idea of the modern-day helicopter date back to this ancient time, and the most famous are the drawings of Leonardo da Vinci, who had this sketch of an "aerial screw." This particular and peculiar concept had a wide screw-shaped propeller on top that would create the lift necessary to lift the user from the ground, but nothing to stop them from continually spinning.

© Mark Rollins 2024
M. Rollins, *The Ultimate LEGO Technic Book*, Maker Innovations Series,
https://doi.org/10.1007/979-8-8688-0793-0_6

**Figure 6-1.** *Leonardo Da Vinci's early helicopter idea, from his sketches*

There were other advancements in this type of vertical takeoff technology, such as Enirco Forlanini, who actually created an unmanned helicopter powered by a steam engine, rising over 40 feet for about 20 seconds. This was in 1877, almost a quarter century before the Wright brothers, and even Thomas Edison himself was not able to create a working helicopter, and part of it was simply due to the horsepower required to get the rotors working to achieve lift.

# How a Helicopter Works

Most helicopters have a main rotor on top, and its spinning allows for the generating of lift to allow the craft to leave the ground. Of course, it takes more than just one giant propeller, which is why the tail rotor is there to compensate for the torque. These things combined will allow for control of a helicopter on the z axis, as well as the x axis and y axis.

# Creating a LEGO Technic Helicopter

Unfortunately, the LEGO Technic helicopter will not be able to be controlled so it will hover and fly through the air. I'm not certain why that is, but I suppose that if LEGO could create that, one would hope that it would be safe. After all, the spinning rotors atop a helicopter could do a lot of damage even in miniaturized form.

The LEGO helicopter that is shown in this particular chapter really has a spinning rotor up top and then a small tail rotor. There is no reason to have them being controlled by a controller, just a battery pack that has on/off functionality.

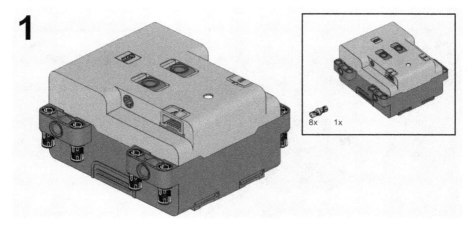

***Figure 6-2.*** *Attach the connector pegs to the battery 9V battery box*

**2**

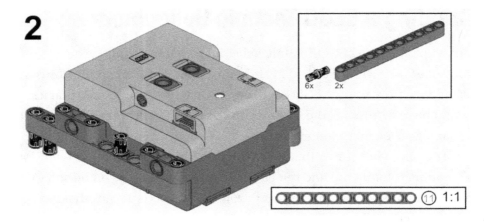

***Figure 6-3.*** *Attach the 11M beams on the connector pegs*

**3**

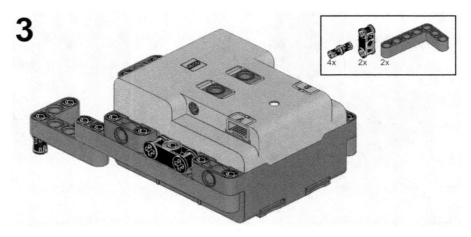

***Figure 6-4.*** *Time to put in the double cross blocks, the 3 × 5 beams, and the connector pegs*

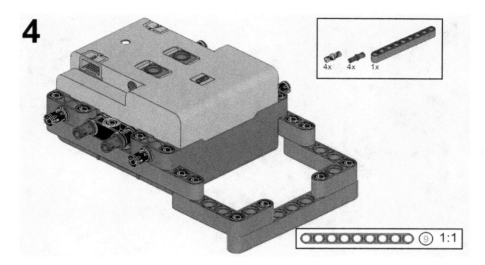

***Figure 6-5.*** *Time to put on the connector peg/cross axles, the connector pegs, and the 9M beam*

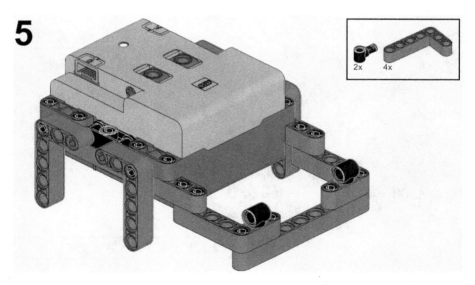

***Figure 6-6.*** *Put on the 3 × 5 beam and the pin with pin hole pieces*

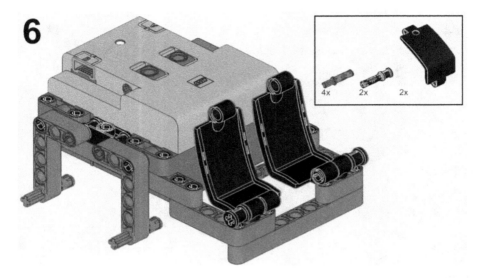

***Figure 6-7.*** *Put on the axle 1M with pin 2M and the pin 3M with friction ridges and stop bush, along with the panel curved 3 × 5 × 3 for seats*

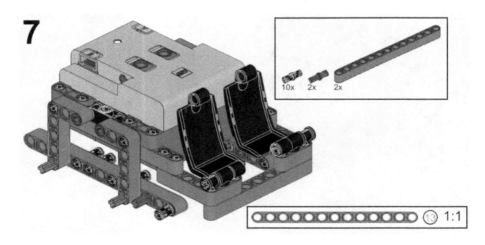

***Figure 6-8.*** *Put on the 13M beams, the connector pegs, and the connector peg/cross axles*

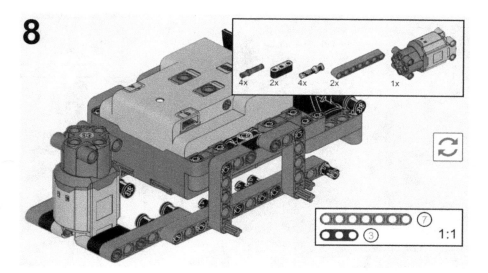

*Figure 6-9.* Put on the 9V electric motor, with the 3M connector pegs, the pin 3M with friction ridges, the 3M beams, and the 7M beams

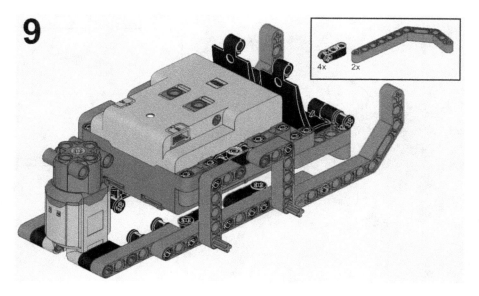

*Figure 6-10.* Put on the 3M cross blocks with axle holes and the two double bent beams

177

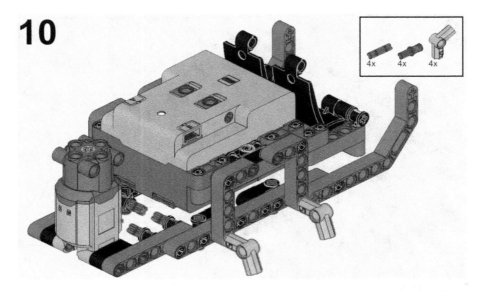

***Figure 6-11.*** *Time to put on the #5 angle elements on and then the 2M axles and connector peg with cross axles*

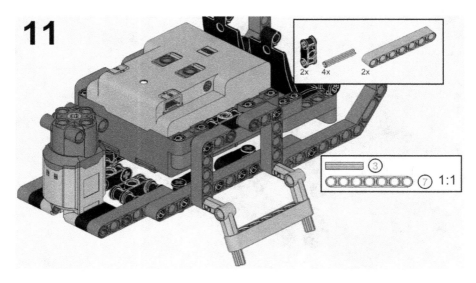

***Figure 6-12.*** *Put on the double cross blocks and the 3M axles, sliding on the 7M beams on each side*

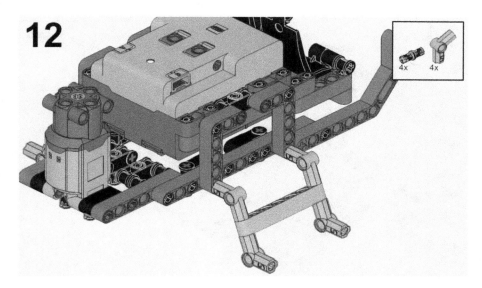

***Figure 6-13.*** *Insert the #5 angle connectors along with the connector pegs*

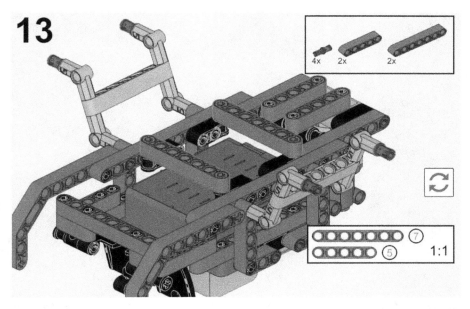

***Figure 6-14.*** *Insert the connector peg/cross axles. Don't forget about the 5M and 7M beams*

**14**

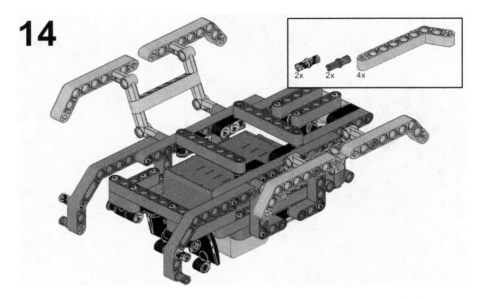

*Figure 6-15.* *Put on the connector pegs and connector peg/cross axles*

**15**

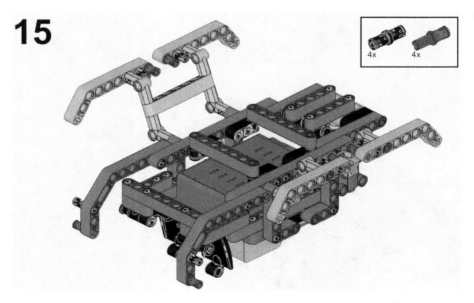

*Figure 6-16.* *Put on the connector pegs and connector peg with cross axles as shown*

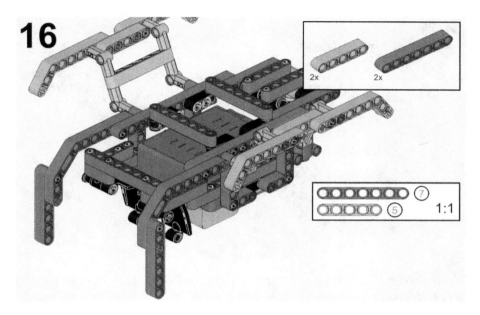

*Figure 6-17.* Put on the 5M and 7M beams

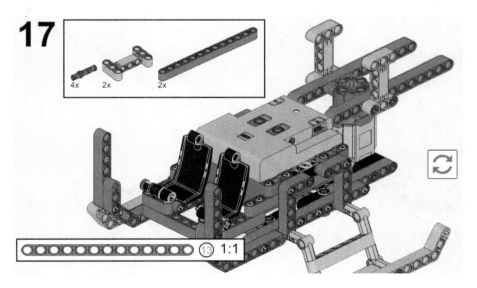

*Figure 6-18.* Use the 3M connector pegs to attach the 13M beams and the H-shape 3 × 5 perpendicular beams

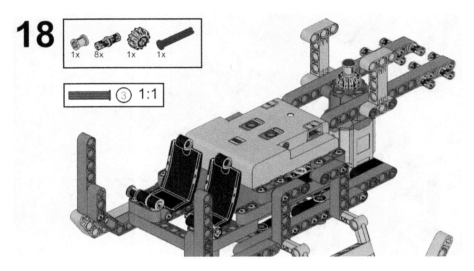

*Figure 6-19.* *Put on the connector pegs and the gear 12 tooth double bevel, the 3M axle with stop, and the bush*

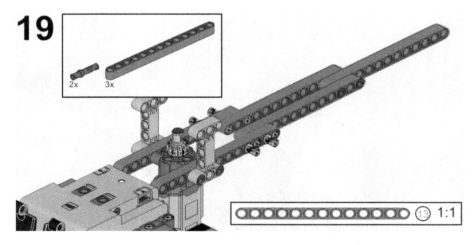

*Figure 6-20.* *Put on the 13M beams with the 3M connector pegs*

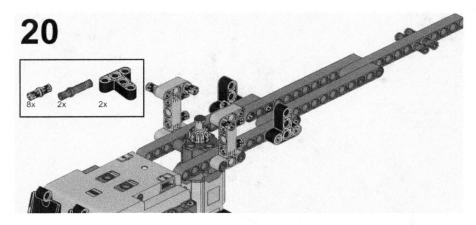

*Figure 6-21.* *Put on the connector pegs, the 3M connector pegs, and T-beams*

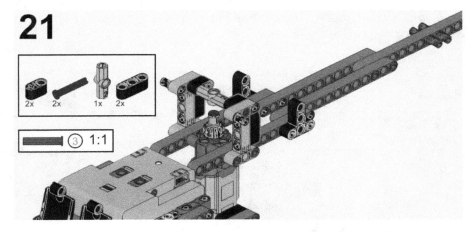

*Figure 6-22.* *Put on the 2M beams with axle, and use the 3M axles with stop and #2 angle connector to hold it together. Don't forget to put on the 3M beams*

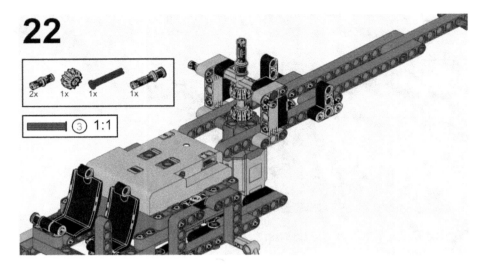

*Figure 6-23.*  *Put on the connector pegs. On top, put on the 3M axle with stop, the 12-tooth gear double bevel, and the pin 3M friction ridges and stop bush*

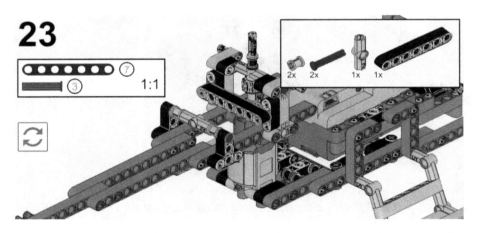

*Figure 6-24.*  *Put on the 7M beam. Use the 3M axles with stops and bushes to secure the #2 angle connector into place*

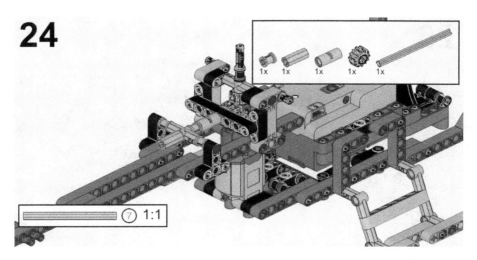

*Figure 6-25.* Put on the 7M axle, with the double bevel 12-tooth gear, the 2M tube, bush, and the 2M axle connector

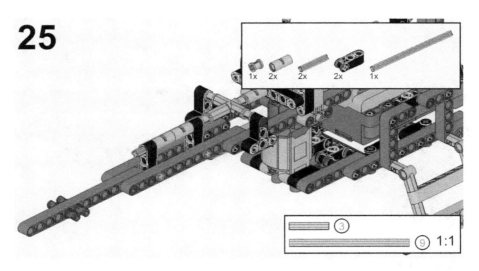

*Figure 6-26.* Put on the 9M axle, the 2M tubes, and the bush. Use the 3M cross block with axle hole, and then use the 3M axles to secure it

**26**

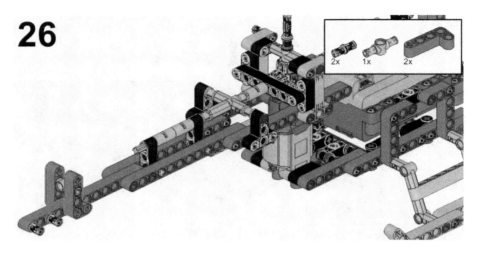

*Figure 6-27.* *Put on the connector pegs, and then put on the 2 × 4 beams with the pin 3M with friction ridges and center pin hole*

**27**

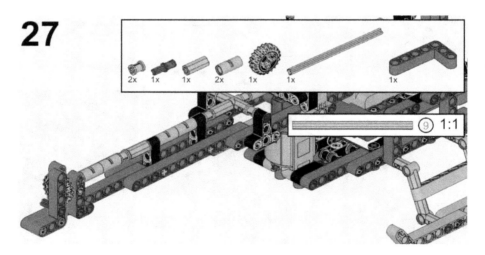

*Figure 6-28.* *Use the 9M beam with the bushes, 2M tubes, axle connector, and the 20-tooth gear double bevel. Use the 3 × 5 beam with connector peg/cross axles*

**28**

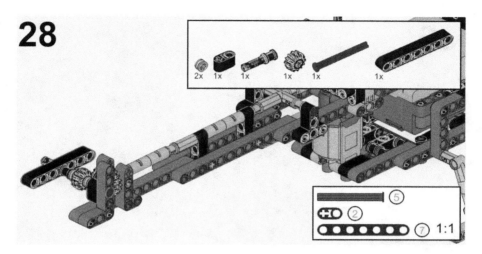

*Figure 6-29.* Put on the 2M with axle hole, with the 5M axle with stop, the friction snap, the 12-tooth double bevel gear, the half bushes, and the 7M beam

**29**

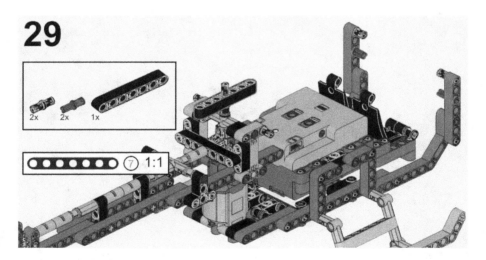

*Figure 6-30.* Use the connector pegs and connector peg/cross axles, with the 7M beam on top

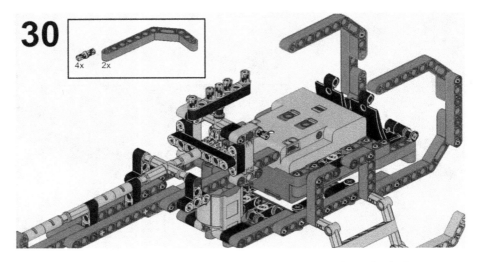

*Figure 6-31.* Use the connector pegs with the double angle beams

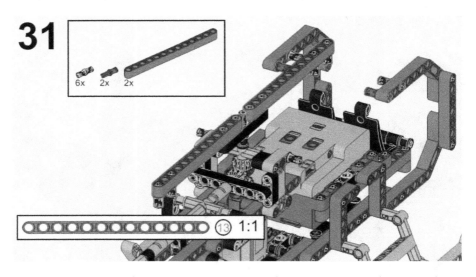

*Figure 6-32.* Use the connector pegs and connector peg/cross axles and the 13M beams

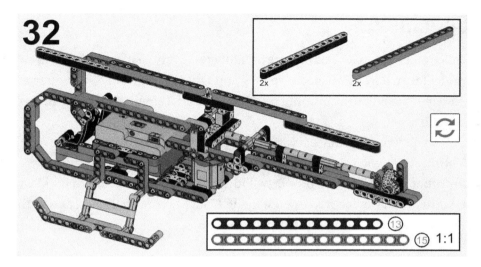

***Figure 6-33.*** *Put on the 13M and 15M beams*

That's pretty much how to make a helicopter in a nutshell, and you can see that it is pretty easy to essentially link a motor for the top rotor and then make an offshoot with LEGO Technic gears and axle to make a side rotor.

I want to make one thing of note. When I constructed this helicopter with my actual LEGO Technic pieces, I used a motor that was 8M in length, and it was one that I could not find on Stud.io as a representative for these instructions. You might discover that as you build this, because the motor that I did use is incompatible with this battery box. I realize that this goes without saying, but you will need to adapt your motor and battery box for these instructions.

# Conclusion

Helicopters in LEGO Technic are actually relatively easy to replicate in model form. Part of it is because they can't fly at this point, so all you really need to do is create a spinning rotor on top and a smaller spinning rotor on the side.

So yeah, that's really easy, right? Well, not quite, because it's LEGO Technic. It's a good time to learn about gears and mechanisms, just like any other LEGO Technic property. Either way, the helicopter is a good way to learn about how to make some flying LEGO Technic vehicles, and in the next chapter, we learn about airplanes.

# CHAPTER 7

# Airplanes

Long before the Wright brothers, humanity dreamed of flying. Of course, the Wright brothers never did believe the man who said: "If God had intended man to fly, He would have given him wings." In case you are not aware, the man who said that was Bishop Wright, the father of Wilbur and Orville. Yes, the boys disproved their old man a few years later, by making their own set of wings.

In all honesty, there has been a great number of LEGO Technic four-wheeled vehicles compared to the number of LEGO Technic planes. Sadly, these LEGO Technic planes do not fly, but if they are built correctly, they can do a lot of other things that LEGO planes cannot do.

This chapter will instruct you on how to create a LEGO plane with all kinds of moving parts, and I'm not just talking about the propeller. This is definitely one of the more complex designs, and I will encourage you discover new ways to make parts.

## Parts of a Plane

Most of you are pretty aware of such common terms like the cockpit and landing gear, not to mention the wings. The wings of a plane are designed to mimic those of the birds, as the wings have a different distance across the top and bottom of the wing, which forces the surrounding air on top to move faster than the air underneath. With the fast-moving air causing pressure to decrease, this means that the air pressure beneath the wings is greater.

© Mark Rollins 2024
M. Rollins, *The Ultimate LEGO Technic Book*, Maker Innovations Series,
https://doi.org/10.1007/979-8-8688-0793-0_7

This creates lift, which brings the plane into the air, as it is greater than gravity, the force that will normally bring a plane down. There are two other forces in balance as a plane is in straight and level flight. The first is thrust, the force that moves an airplane forward, which is generated by the jet engines or propeller. Then there is drag, the air resistance that will slow the movement of an airplane.

Of course, there is more than just keeping forces in balance to maintain a steady flight, but it also is required to have a mastery of turning while in the air, not to mention ascension and descension. This is where the parts of an aircraft come in.

There are two sections of the wings on a plane that can control lift and direction. One of them are the flaps, located closest to the center of the plane, which are made to move symmetrically to create more lift and drag, and used during takeoff and landing. This is when the airspeeds are lower and used for additional lift and reduction of stall speeds.

Then there are also the ailerons, which are located on the trailing edge of the wing in order to help control the roll of a plane. For example, a pilot turning right will cause the right aileron to go up reducing lift on that side, with the left aileron going down, increasing the lift so that side will rise.

That tail section also has sections to help maintain the stability of a plan in flight. The first is the horizontal stabilizer, made to keep the airplane's nose from moving up and down. On this section is an elevator, and when that elevator goes up, it causes more force to push down on the tail, resulting in the raising of the aircraft's nose. This also has the effect of changing the angle of the wings, resulting in more lift.

The tail is also the home of the vertical stabilizer, which helps to prevent a side-to-side motion of the airplane's nose. The rudder is controlled at the cockpit using left and right pedals, with the left pedal deflecting the rudder to the left, pushing the tail right, and the nose to go left. These are good for turns.

# Construction of a LEGO Technic Plane

For this next set of instructions, which will be quite long, I am going to go through how to create a plane with certain steps. Just to let you know, this model is not really designed based on any actual plane, but merely to show how to create a plane and its separate parts.

You will note that there is a battery pack, which only operates the propeller. As for all of the other features, I show how to create special levers and gears that allow certain parts to move. I felt no need to motorize them because if you were to try and operate them while the plane is in your hand, it is just easier to use your other hand on the controls, rather than a remote.

Now, can you make these parts motorized? Sure. It gets pretty complex, and so I will leave that up to you. I will cover the construction of the tail with its rudder and elevators and the wings with the ailerons and flaps. However, I want to start with something that many of the bigger jumbo jets have retractable landing gear.

# Retractable Landing Gear

With these first steps, you will create the bottom section of the plane, which includes an axle connector in step 10 that, when rotated, will cause the three landing gears to retract or deploy all at the same time.

Just to let you know, I had to take a page from LEGO's Technic set 9394 to get this to work. For me, I found it quite challenging to create the retraction feature, because you have to account for the direction it goes up and down, and it is harder than it looks, believe me. I also borrowed the idea of using these levers for controls, but I assure you that the designs of the flaps and ailerons are all me.

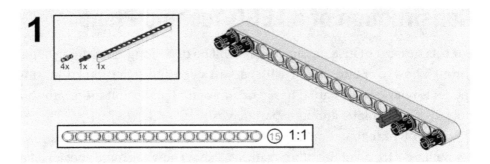

***Figure 7-1.*** *Put the four connector pegs and the connector peg with cross axle on the 15M beam*

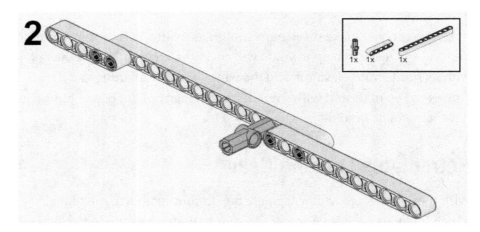

***Figure 7-2.*** *Put on the 5M and 11M beams, along with the angle connector #2*

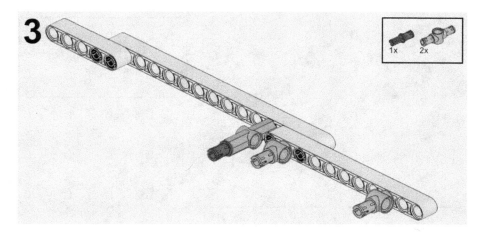

***Figure 7-3.*** *Put on the connector peg with axle and the 3M peg with center through hole*

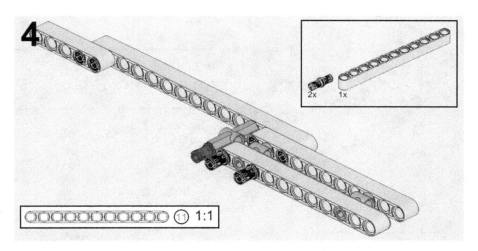

***Figure 7-4.*** *Put on another 11M beam, along with the two connector pegs*

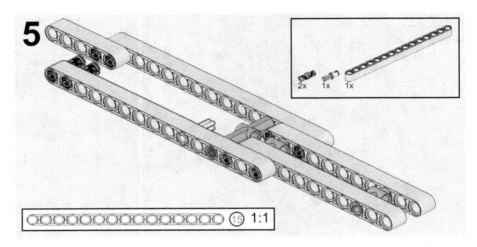

***Figure 7-5.*** *Time for another 15M beam with a connector peg with axle without friction ridges. Don't forget about the other two connector pegs*

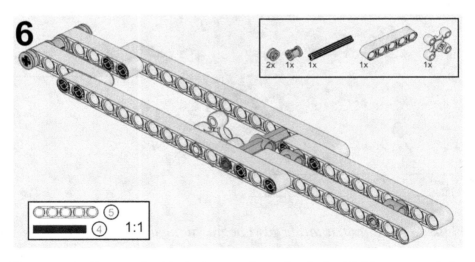

***Figure 7-6.*** *Put on the Technic angular wheel, the 5M beam, and the 4M axle with the bushes and half bushes*

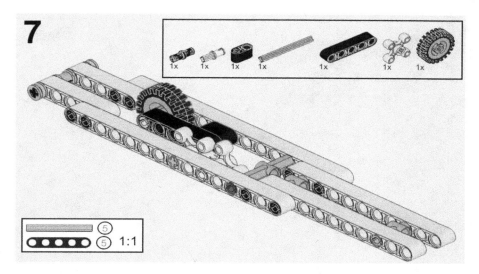

***Figure 7-7.*** *You'll need to line up the Technic angular wheel with the 5M axle. Put in the 5M beam, with the connector peg and 2M beam with axle hole. Insert the connector peg/cross axle with the wheel*

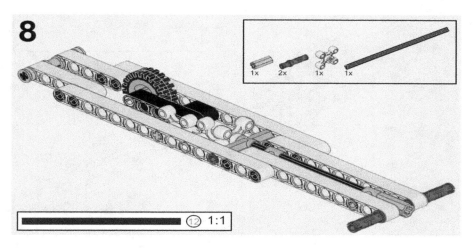

***Figure 7-8.*** *Put on the 12M axle and the Technic angular wheel to mesh perpendicular with the others, capping it off with the axle connector. Put on the 3M connector pegs*

197

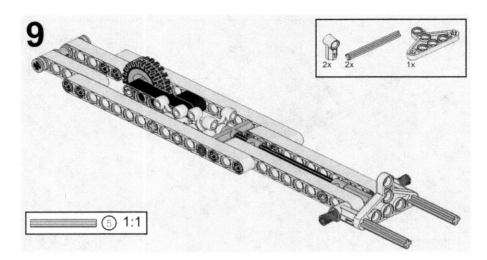

**Figure 7-9.** *Slide on the #1 angle connector, and then insert the 5M axles, followed by the Technic triangle*

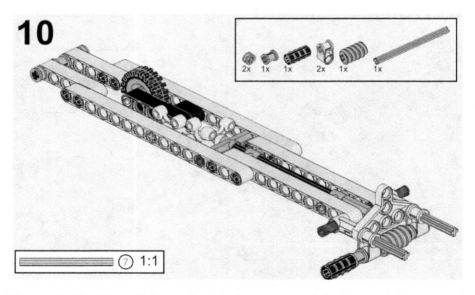

**Figure 7-10.** *First slide on the 90-degree cross blocks, and then put on the worm gear, half bushes, bush, and axle connector*

198

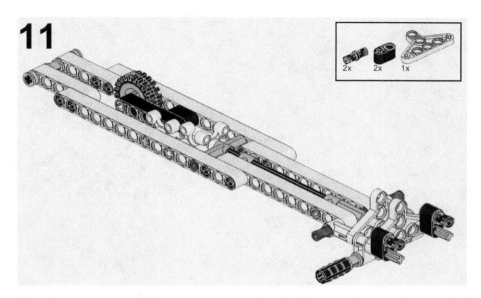

*Figure 7-11.* *Put on the Technic triangle, as well as the 2M beam with cross axle and the connector pegs*

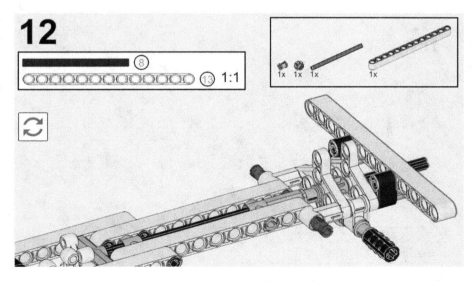

*Figure 7-12.* *Put on the 8M axle with the bush, making certain that the 8-tooth gear meshes with the worm gear. Put on the 13M beam*

199

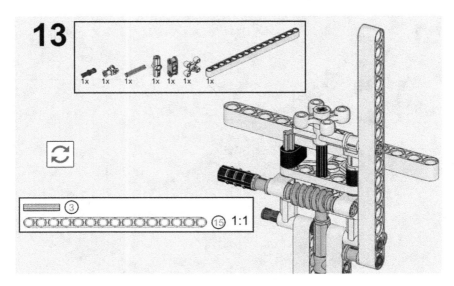

***Figure 7-13.*** *Put on the 15M beam with the connector peg/cross axle and the double cross block. Put on the 3M axle with #2 angle connector and 90-degree axle connector, with the angular wheel on as shown*

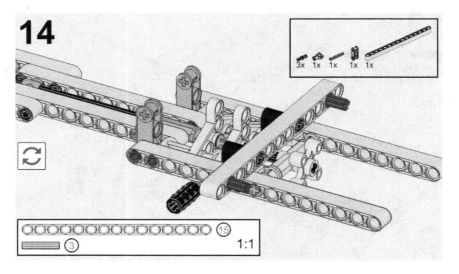

***Figure 7-14.*** *Use the 3M axle with 90-degree angle connector, and use the 15M beam, the three connector peg/cross axles, and the double cross block*

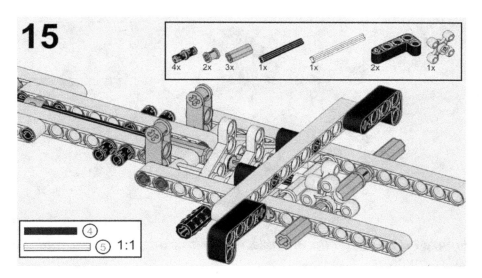

**Figure 7-15.** *Use the 4M and 5M axles, the bushes, and the axle connectors, to mesh the Technic angular wheel as shown. Put on the 2 × 4 beams*

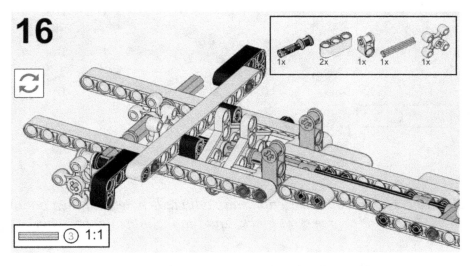

**Figure 7-16.** *Put on the friction peg with axle, the 90-degree cross block, and the 3M axle with angular wheel. Go ahead and put on the 3M beams on the side*

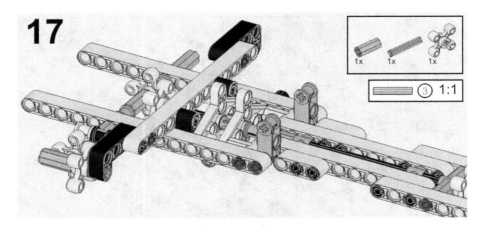

***Figure 7-17.*** *Put on the 3M axle, the Technic angular wheel, and the axle connector*

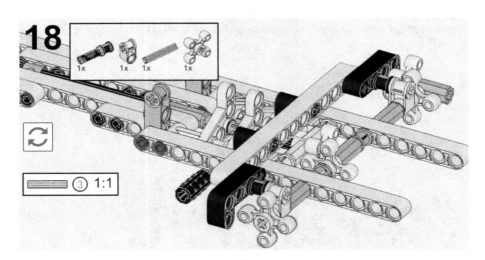

***Figure 7-18.*** *Put on the friction snap with axle hole, and then put on the 3M axle, 90-degree cross block, and the Technic angular wheel*

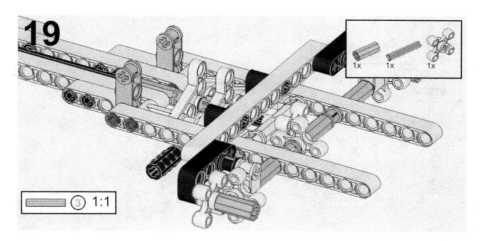

***Figure 7-19.*** *Put on the 3M axle, the Technic angular wheel, and the axle connector*

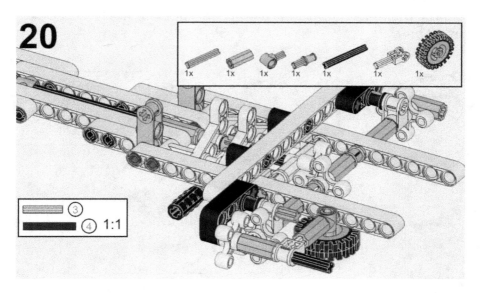

***Figure 7-20.*** *Put on the 3M axle, and then put on the 4M axle, the 2M axle with handle axle connector, the axle with pin hole, connector peg without friction, and then the wheel with split axle hole with black tire 24 mm*

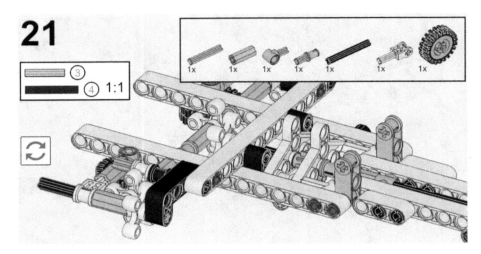

*Figure 7-21.* Put on the 3M axle, and then put on the 4M axle, the 2M axle with handle axle connector, the axle with pin hole, connector peg without friction, and then the wheel with split axle hole with black tire 24 mm

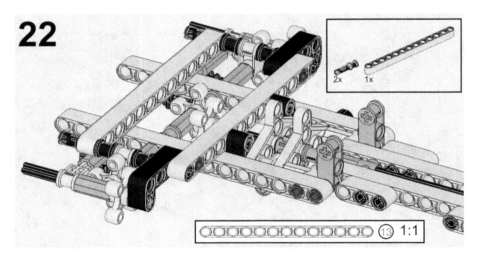

*Figure 7-22.* Use the fiction snaps with cross axle to attach the 13M beam

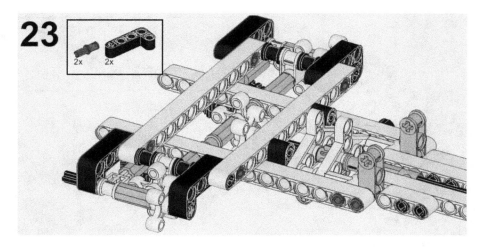

***Figure 7-23.*** *Put on the connector peg/cross axles, securing them with the 2 × 4 beams*

Now, if you do this part right, there is an axle connector in step 10 that, if turned, will retract or extend the landing gear. Try it out for yourself.

## The Airplane Body with Elevators

These next few steps are going to highlight creating a body of a plane, with the application of elevators on the first part of the tail section. Just to let you know, these aren't really how elevators work on some planes, but it creates a tail section that can tilt like them. There is even a lever to control them.

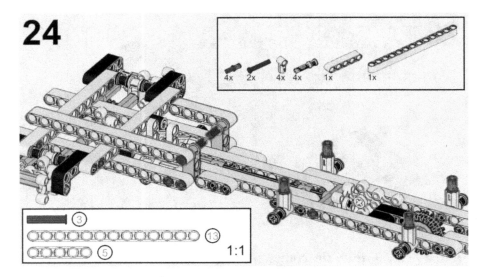

**Figure 7-24.** *Use the fiction snaps with the #1 angle connectors and the connector pegs/cross axles. Use the two 3M axles with stop with the 5M and 13M beams*

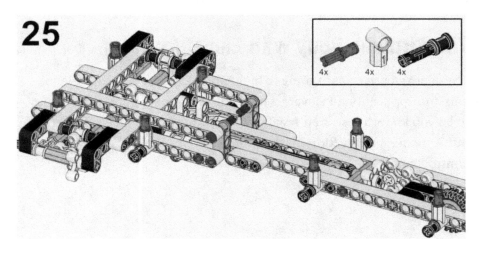

**Figure 7-25.** *Use the fiction snaps with the #1 angle connectors and the connector pegs/cross axles*

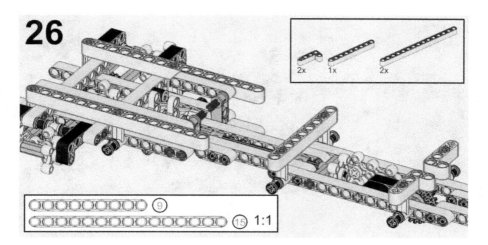

*Figure 7-26.* Attach the 2 × 4 beams, along with the 9M and
15M beams

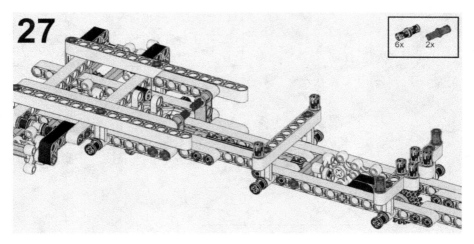

*Figure 7-27.* Put on the six connector pegs with the two connector
pegs/cross axles

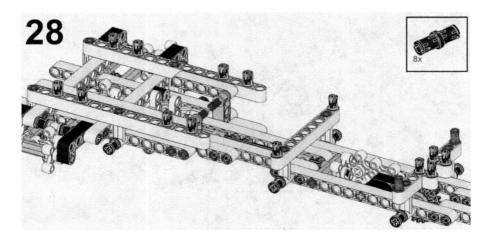

*Figure 7-28.* *Put on the eight connector pegs as shown*

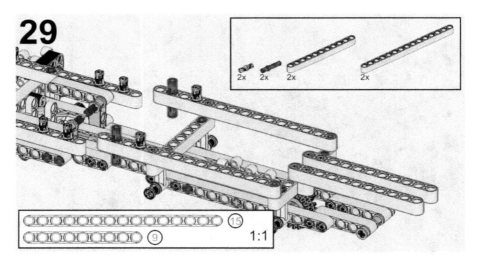

*Figure 7-29.* *Put on the 9M and 15M beams with two connector pegs and two 3M connector pegs*

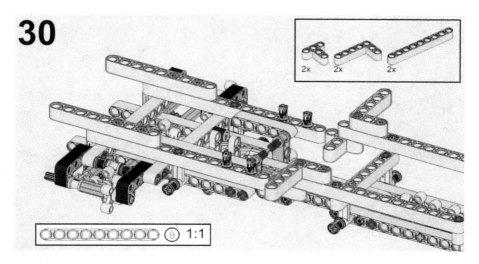

**Figure 7-30.** *Put on the two 9M beams, the two 3 × 5 beams, and the two 3 × 3 T-beams*

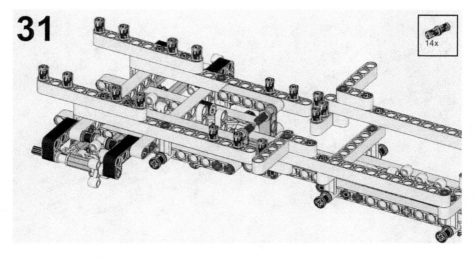

**Figure 7-31.** *Put on the 14 connector pegs*

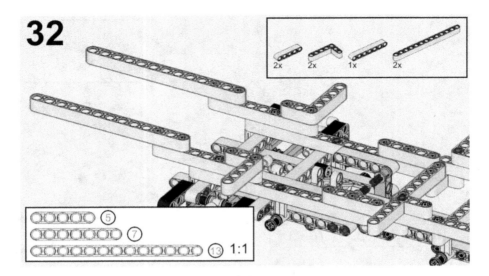

*Figure 7-32.* Put on the 5M, 7M, and 13M beams and the two 3 × 5 beams

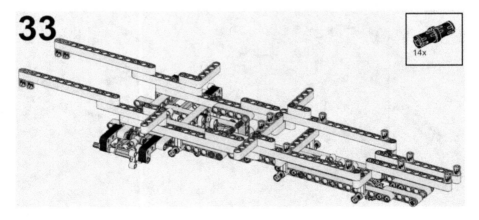

*Figure 7-33.* Put on the 14 connector pegs

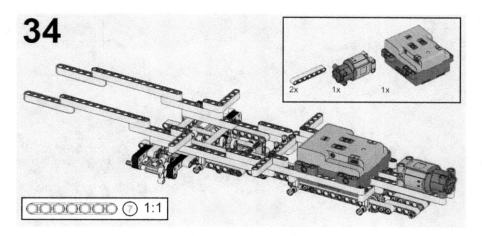

*Figure 7-34.* Put on the 7M beams, as well as the 9V battery box and the 9V motor

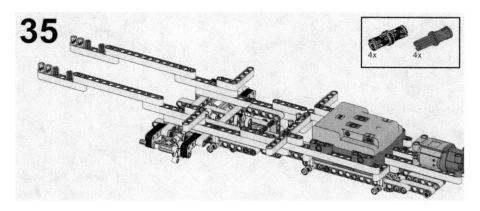

*Figure 7-35.* Put on the four connector pegs with the four connector pegs/cross axles

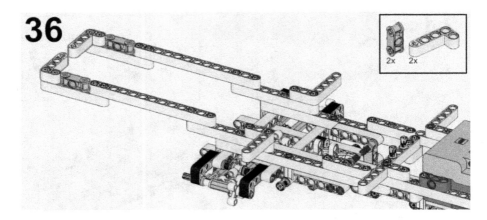

*Figure 7-36.* *Put on the two 2 × 4 beams and the two double cross blocks*

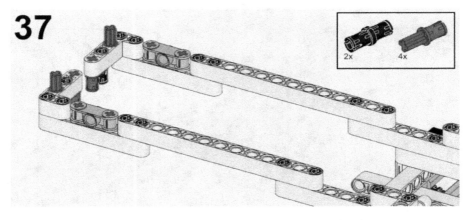

*Figure 7-37.* *Put on the two connector pegs with the four connector pegs/cross axles*

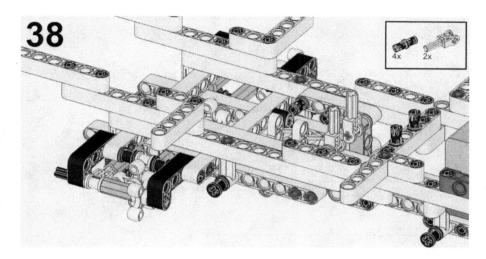

*Figure 7-38.* Put on the four connector pegs with the two axles/
reverse handles

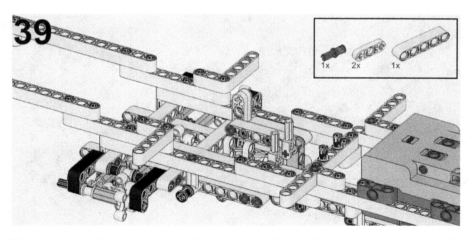

*Figure 7-39.* Put on the 5M beam, attaching the two 3M levers and
connector peg/cross axle

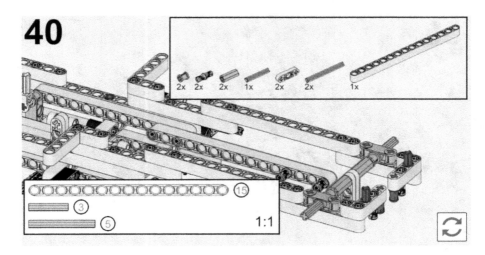

*Figure 7-40.* *Put on the 15M beam with two connector pegs. Use the 3M axle on the 3M levers, with axle connectors, 5M axles, and bushes*

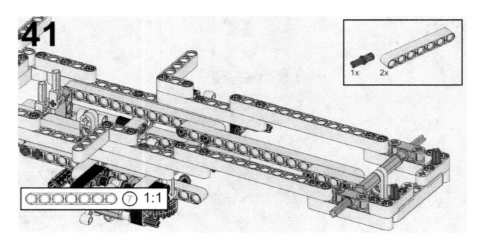

*Figure 7-41.* *Put on the two 7M beams and use the connector peg/ cross axle to link it*

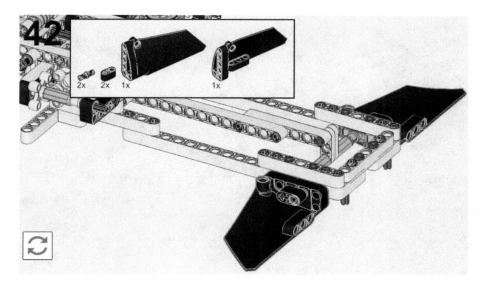

***Figure 7-42.*** *Click on the #17 and #18 panels, securing them with the connector pegs and 2M beams with cross axle*

All right, now that you have this elevator portion, you can see that they will slightly rotate if you pull the lever in the front, which is on the cockpit on the right. Time for the next portion.

## The Left Wing Aileron and Flap

This next portion is about how to do the flap and the aileron on the left side, with the flaps moving in sync and then the aileron on its own.

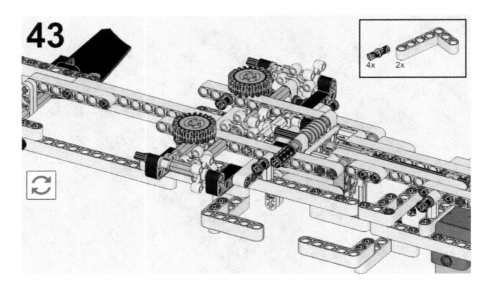

***Figure 7-43.*** *Connect the two 3 × 5 beams with the four connector pegs*

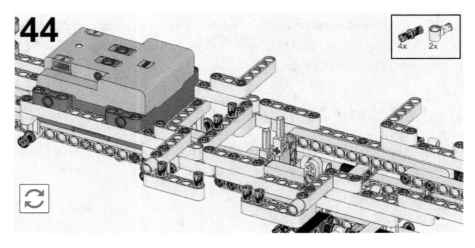

***Figure 7-44.*** *Put in the four connector pegs with the two Technic pegs with through hole*

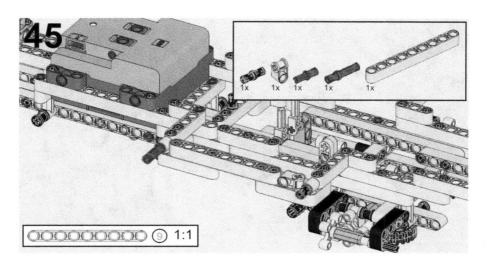

**Figure 7-45.** *Use the 90-degree cross block, the connector peg/ cross axle, and the 9M beam, and add the 3M connector peg and connector peg*

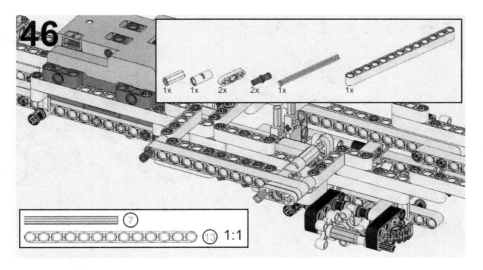

**Figure 7-46.** *Use the 13M beam, and then use the 7M axle with the 3M levers, the tube, and axle connector*

217

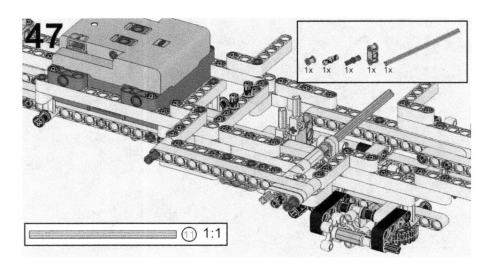

**Figure 7-47.** *Put on the 11M axle with the bush. Connect the double cross block and then use the connector peg and connector peg/ cross axle*

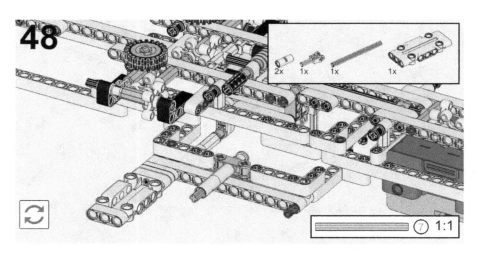

**Figure 7-48.** *Use the 7M axle and the two tubes, with the 2M axle reverser. Then put on the 3 × 7 × 1 panel*

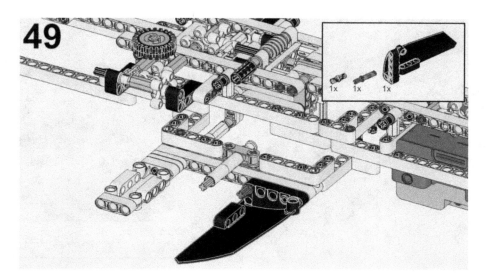

**Figure 7-49.** Use the connector peg and 2M connector peg with 1M axle with #18 panel

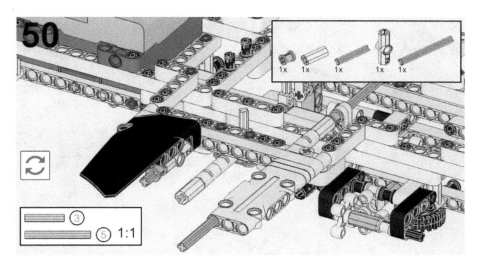

**Figure 7-50.** Use the 5M axle on the panel, the axle connector, and the #2 angle connector with 3M axle and bush

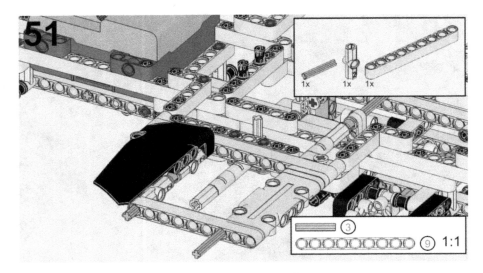

***Figure 7-51.*** *Use the 3M axle with the #2 angle connector and then the 9M beam*

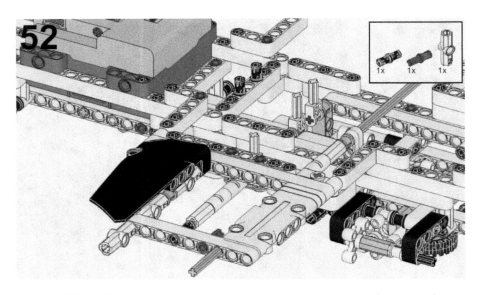

***Figure 7-52.*** *Use the connector peg and connector peg/cross axle, and then use the #2 angle connector*

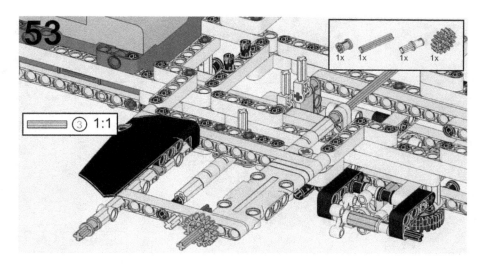

**Figure 7-53.** *Put on the bush with the 3M axle, and then insert the connector peg/cross axle (without friction) and the 16-tooth gear*

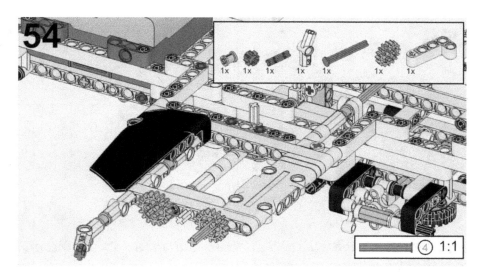

**Figure 7-54.** *Put on the 2 × 4 beam and then link it with the 4M axle with stop with 8-tooth gear and bush. Put on the #3 angle connector with 2M axle and the 16-tooth gear*

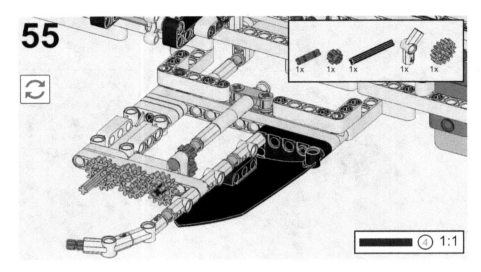

***Figure 7-55.*** *Use the 4M axle to join the 8-tooth gear and 16-tooth gear. Connect the #4 angle connector with the 2M axle*

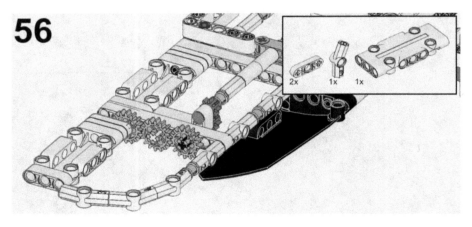

***Figure 7-56.*** *Connect the two 3M levers with the 3 × 7 × 1 panel and then the #3 angle connector*

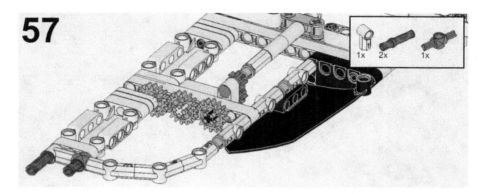

***Figure 7-57.*** *Put on the #1 angle connector with the 3M connector peg, along with the axle and peg connector with two axles*

You will know if you did this section right if you pull on the lever on the left of the cockpit, and the flap will move. There is a lever on the wing that you can pull and the aileron will move. Now, it is time to do the other side.

## The Right Wing Aileron and Flap

This next portion is about how to do the flap and the aileron on the right side, with the flaps moving in sync and then the aileron on its own.

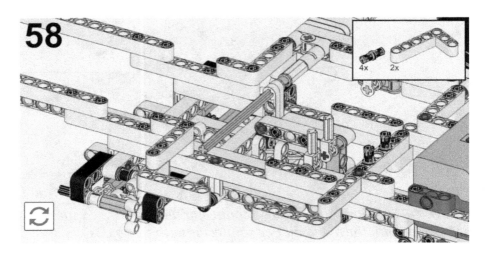

***Figure 7-58.*** *Connect the two 3 × 5 beams with the four connector pegs*

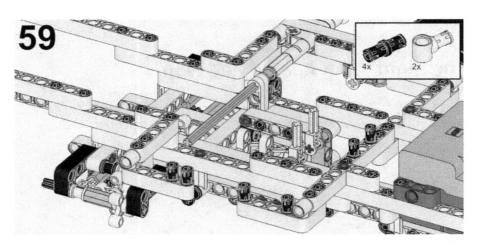

***Figure 7-59.*** *Put in the four connector pegs with the two Technic pegs with through hole*

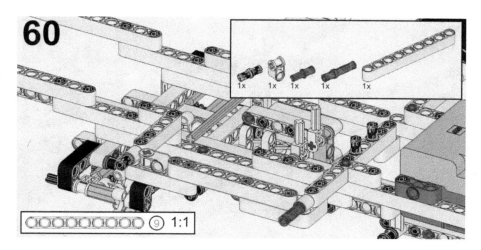

***Figure 7-60.*** *Use the 90-degree cross block, the connector peg/ cross axle, and the 9M beam, and add the 3M connector peg and connector peg*

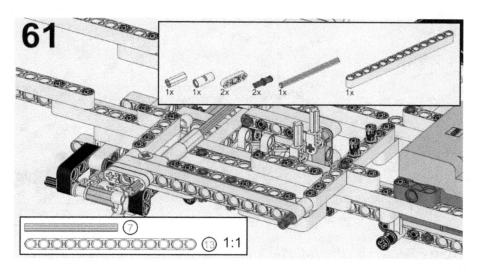

***Figure 7-61.*** *Use the 13M beam, and then use the 7M ale with the 3M levers, the tube, and axle connector*

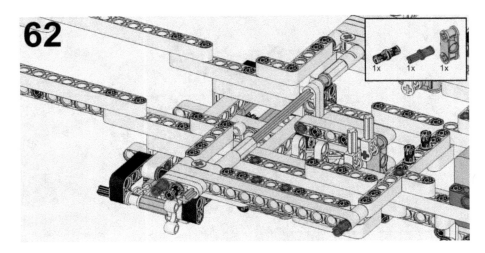

***Figure 7-62.*** *Connect the double cross block and then use the connector peg and connector peg/cross axle*

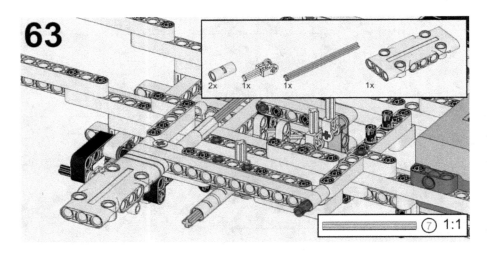

***Figure 7-63.*** *Use the 7M axle and the two tubes, with the 2M axle reversers. Then put on the 3 × 7 × 1 panel*

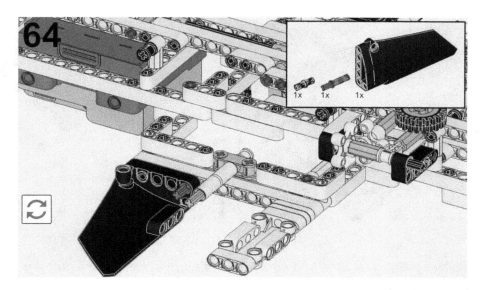

***Figure 7-64.*** *Use the connector peg and 2M connector peg with 1M axle with #17 panel*

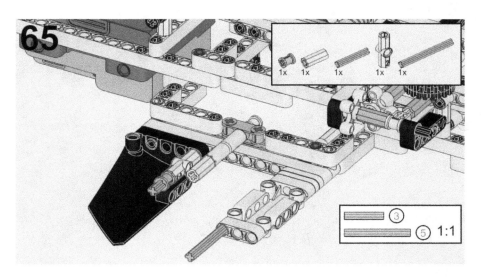

***Figure 7-65.*** *Use the 5M axle on the panel, the axle connector, and the #2 angle connector with 3M axle and bush*

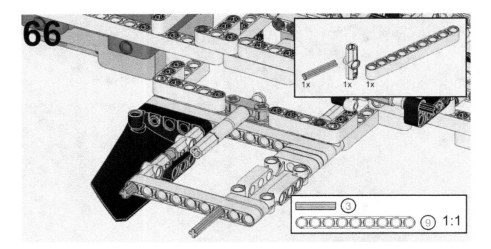

***Figure 7-66.*** *Use the 3M axle with the #2 angle connector and then the 9M beam*

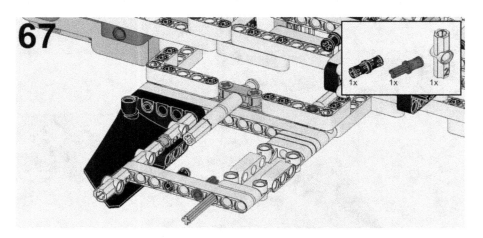

***Figure 7-67.*** *Use the connector peg and connector peg/cross axle, and then use the #2 angle connector*

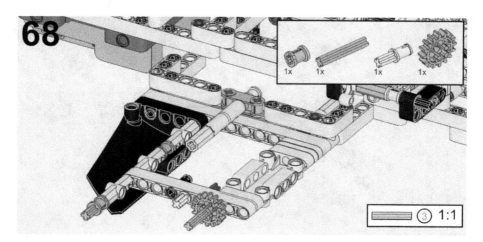

*Figure 7-68.* *Put on the bush with the 3M axle, and then insert the connector peg/cross axle (without friction) and the 16-tooth gear*

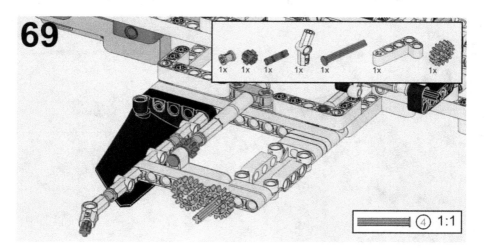

*Figure 7-69.* *Put on the 2 × 4 beam and then link it with the 4M axle with stop with 8-tooth gear and bush. Put on the #3 angle connector with 2M axle and the 16-tooth gear*

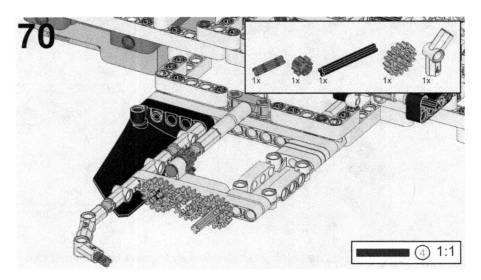

***Figure 7-70.*** *Use the 4M axle to join the 8-tooth gear and 16-tooth gear. Connect the #4 angle connector with the 2M axle*

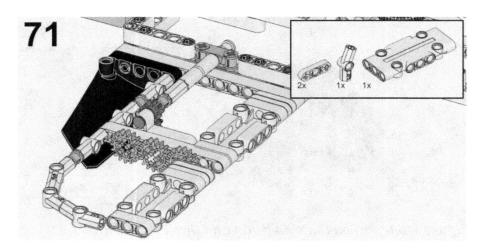

***Figure 7-71.*** *Connect the two 3M levers with the 3 × 7 × 1 panel and then the #3 angle connector*

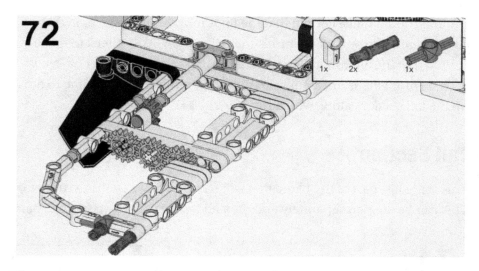

*Figure 7-72.* *Put on the #1 angle connector with the 3M connector peg, along with the axle and peg connector with two axles*

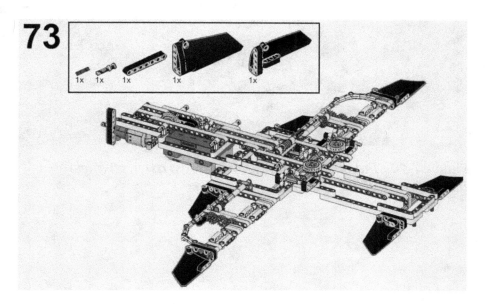

*Figure 7-73.* *Time to put on the #17 and #18 panels. Put on the 2M axle, friction snap with axle, and 7M beam as a propeller*

You should make certain that the flaps move with the lever in the cockpit, near the one that controls the tail section. Also, check to make certain that the aileron moves with the right lever like the left one. Now that the propeller is on, along with the wings ready to go, it is time to finish up the tail section, along with a rudder.

## Tail Section

This is the last part of the plane that will have the fin as well as a rudder. This can be created separately and then added on with the last of the parts.

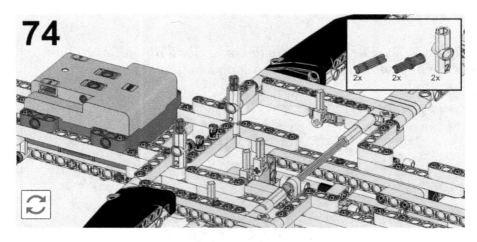

*Figure 7-74.* *Put on the connector pegs/cross axles, #2 angle connectors, and 2M axle*

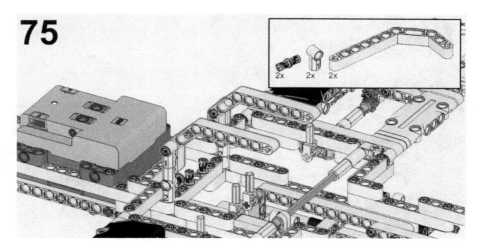

***Figure 7-75.*** *Put on the connector pegs, the #1 angle connectors, the 3M connector pegs, and double bend 90-degree beam*

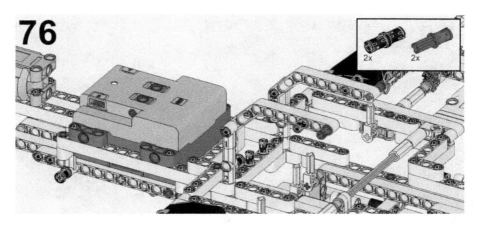

***Figure 7-76.*** *Put on the two connector pegs and connector peg/ cross axles*

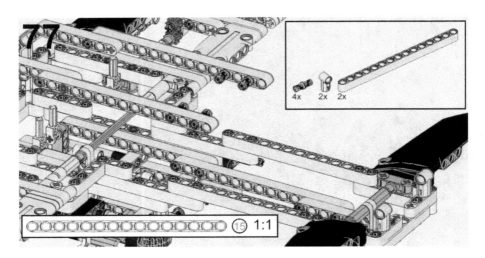

**Figure 7-77.** *Put on the #1 angle connectors, the 15M beams, and the four connector pegs*

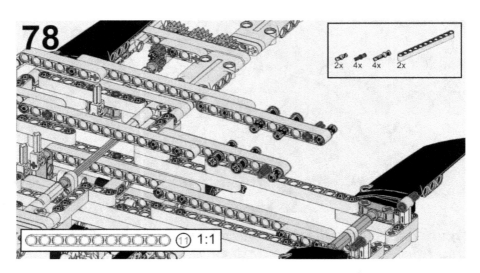

**Figure 7-78.** *Use the four connector pegs, the connector peg/cross axles, the friction snap with cross axles, and the two 11M beams*

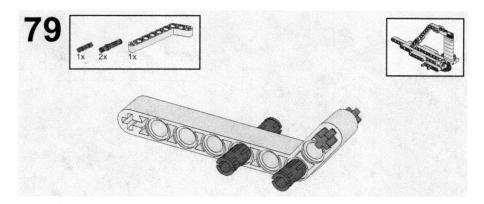

**Figure 7-79.** *On a 3 × 7 beam, put on the two 3M connector pegs and 2M axle*

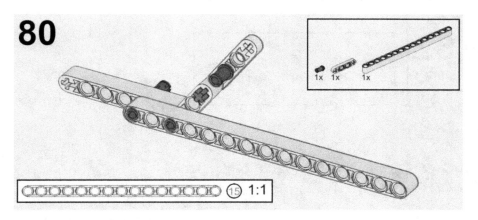

**Figure 7-80.** *Put on the 15M beam, with the 4M lever and the connector peg with stud*

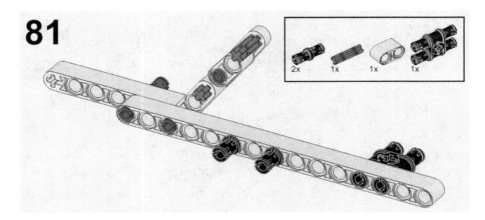

***Figure 7-81.*** *Put on the 2M axle, the connector pegs, the 2M beam, and the double peg with axle hole*

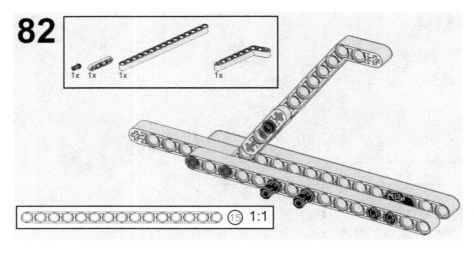

***Figure 7-82.*** *Put on the 15M, with the 3 × 7 beam and the 4M levers and connector peg with stud*

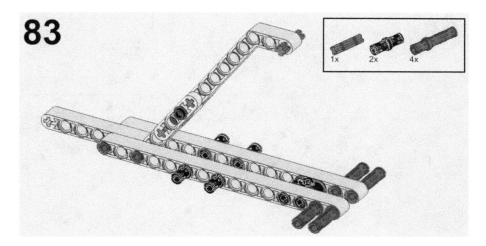

**Figure 7-83.** *Put on the 2M axle, connector pegs, and 3M connector pegs*

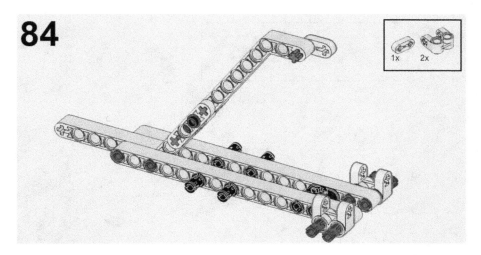

**Figure 7-84.** *Put on the 2M lever and the two axle and peg connector double split*

237

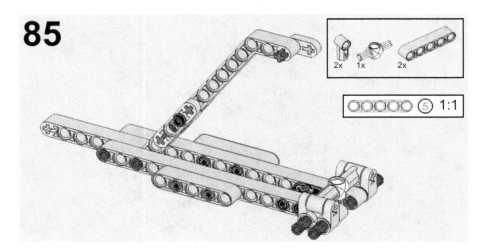

***Figure 7-85.*** *Put on the 5M beams, and connect the axle and peg connector with two axles with the two #1 angle connectors*

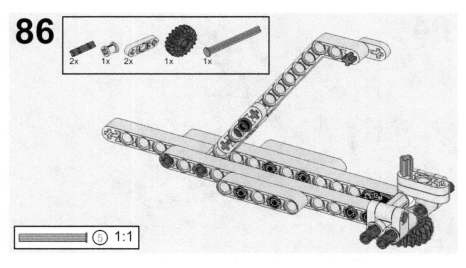

***Figure 7-86.*** *Put on the 2M axles. Then put on the 4M axle with stop, with 3M levers, Technic 20-tooth gear, and the bush*

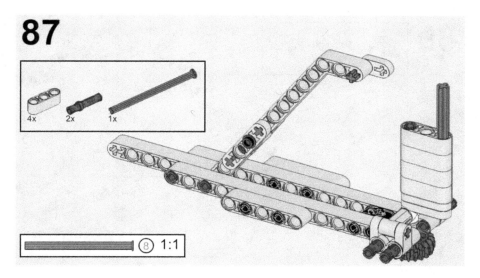

*Figure 7-87.* Put on the 8M axle with stop, and put on the 3M beams and 3M connector pegs

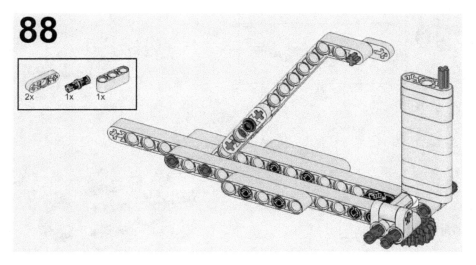

*Figure 7-88.* Put on the 3M beam and the 3M levers, linking them with the connector peg

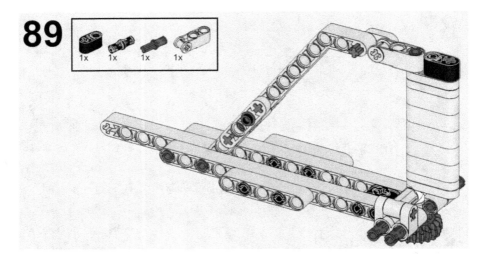

***Figure 7-89.*** *Put on the cross block with two through holes, the connector pegs, the connector peg/cross axles, and the 2M beam with cross axle*

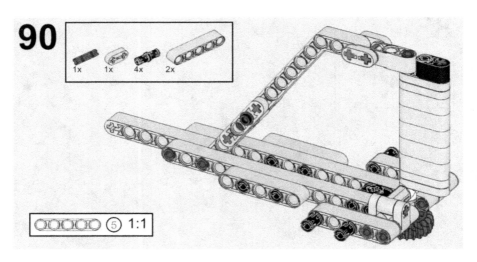

***Figure 7-90.*** *Put on 5M beams and connector pegs. Then put on the 2M lever and the 2M axle*

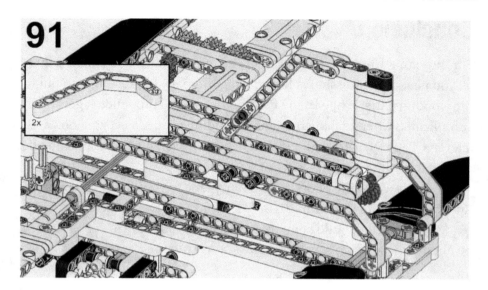

***Figure 7-91.*** *Technic double-bend beams*

Before I wrap up this chapter, I want to make the same disclaimer that I made in the last chapter about helicopters. That is, the motor used to power the propeller might be different than the one that I used here. As it so happens, Stud.io didn't have this newer Power Functions motor, and I had to use one that they did have, which is not compatible to the battery box used in these airplane instructions. In the case of the airplane design, it is a pretty simple fix, requiring a different placement of the connector pegs.

I did keep this design pretty bare bones, simply so you can see how to get the controls down. By controls, I mean the stuff that the levers can manipulate, but most planes do have a shell around them. I figured that you can use the principles about creating an auto body and apply it to the plan if you want to make something that looks even better in the air.

241

# Conclusion

For those that want to create a LEGO Technic airplane, you will find that all you need is a basic shape, but what gets it really interesting is to put in the working parts. While it isn't difficult to add in a propeller, it gets really complicated when making retractable landing gear. Also, if you look at the ailerons, flaps, elevators, and rudder, it can be even more complicated than any vehicle with four wheels.

Still, it is worth the effort to hold that plane in your hand, and you will find that it is quite something. If only it could fly.

Maybe we can't build something that can fly, but the next chapter will be about how to make some interesting construction equipment.

# CHAPTER 8

# Lego Technic Construction Equipment

One thing about Technic pieces is that they are very good at creating machines that can make stuff happen. I talked about it with creating vehicles with steering functions, and now I want to take it a step further and talk about how to make creations like forklifts, scissor lifts, and anything else that you might need to have when you are on a construction site.

Now, before I begin, I want to say that you will learn to build construction equipment, but not all of it. For example, I will show you how to make the lifting part of the forklift, but as far as the whole part with the wheels and frame, I'm just going to tell you that you should review the chapters that I had on making a frame that you can take control of.

## LEGO Technic Forklift

One of the earliest models of Technic, back when it was the Expert sets, was the forklift, and it wasn't motorized, but you could turn a crank to raise up the prongs, and it was all done with the original LEGO Technic bricks and plates.

© Mark Rollins 2024
M. Rollins, *The Ultimate LEGO Technic Book*, Maker Innovations Series,
https://doi.org/10.1007/979-8-8688-0793-0_8

This particular forklift is based on the instructions that I had in one of my LEGO books, using beams and racks, as well as a motor. The one from my book didn't have a motor as it was kind of difficult to motorize it, and I will explain why.

To make a forklift work, at least in this type of design, it requires a rack-and-pinion type mechanism, something that I never felt worked well with motorized steering. Turning a gear to move a rack produces the type of vertical rising movement required to make a forklift a forklift. To do that, that gear has to be put on the top of the structure, but you have to power that to spin, somehow, which was one of the biggest challenges that I had to face.

You will note that it takes a total of eight gears to make this happen, and it was grueling to figure out how to do that, and perhaps you can figure out how to do it in a simpler manner. I actually think that most forklifts use hydraulics to make it work, and I didn't really want to use the chain formation like on some Technic motorcycle sets to make this work. The good news is that the motor weighs down the nonlifting area of the forklift, which is something that you need.

As for how much weight you can lift, I'm going to have to say, not much, and perhaps you can figure out better ways. In fact, if you want to make it go higher, you'll have to figure out how to make longer racks, which could raise higher, but causes issues with the structure.

Speaking of issues with structure, the forklift will jam if the gears are taken too far, and you will hear it. It will rise slowly enough so you can quickly turn off the battery pack where you need to.

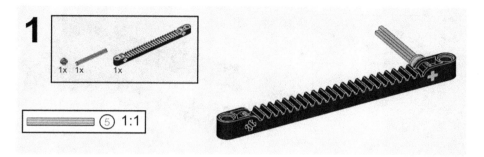

***Figure 8-1.*** *Start with the Technic gear rack 1 × 13, and put in the 5M axle through the side axle hole, and slide on the half bush*

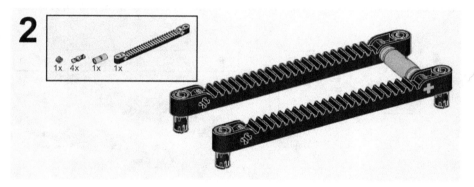

***Figure 8-2.*** *Put on the 2M tube on the axle from the last step, and slide on the half bush and gear rack 1 × 13. Then it is time to insert the four connector pegs in the bottom as shown*

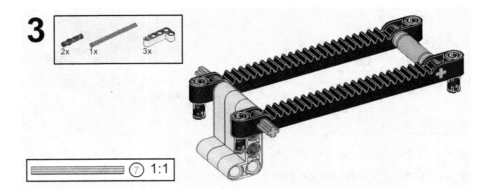

***Figure 8-3.*** *Link up the three 2 × 4 beams with the 3M connector pegs, and then slide on the 7M axle so the beams are in the middle*

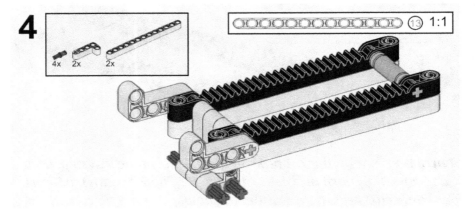

***Figure 8-4.*** *Put on the four connector peg/cross axles on the 2 × 4 beams as shown, and then slide on the 2 × 4 beams on the 7M axles from the last step. On the bottom of the 13M racks, snap on the 13M beams*

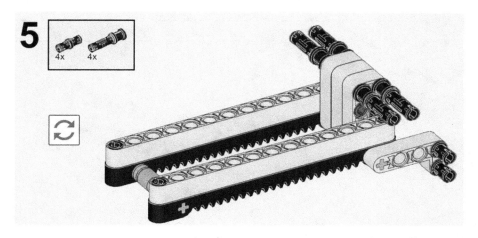

***Figure 8-5.*** *Stick on the 3M peg with friction ridges and then the connector pegs as shown*

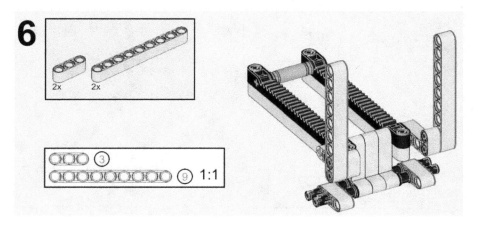

***Figure 8-6.*** *Time to put on the 9M beams, which serve as the prongs for your forklift. And don't forget to put in the 3M beams*

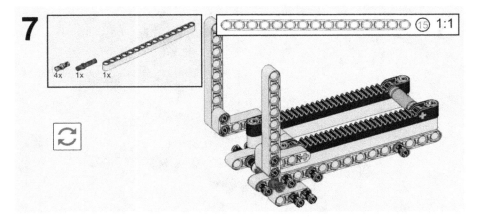

***Figure 8-7.*** *Put on the 15M beam, and then put on the 3M connector pegs and regular-sized connector pegs*

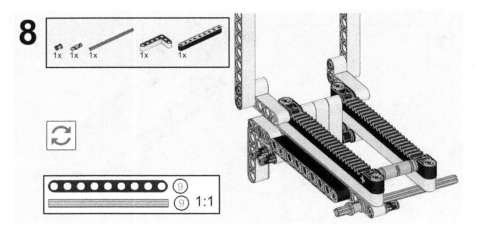

***Figure 8-8.*** *Put on the 9M beam and the 3 × 5 beam. Put on the connector peg and slide on the 9M axle with the bush*

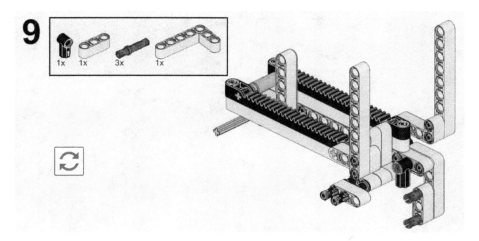

***Figure 8-9.*** *Time to put in the 3M connector pegs and 3M beam. Put on the 3 × 5 on the other side, and put on the #1 angle connector on top*

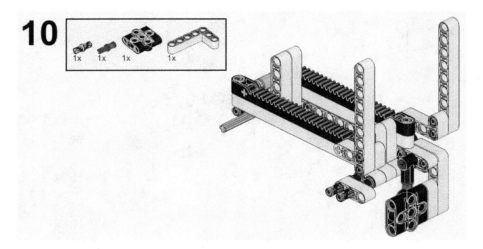

***Figure 8-10.*** *Put on the 3 × 5 beam, and put on the connector peg/ cross axle and connector peg. Put on the connector block 1 × 3 × 3*

**11**

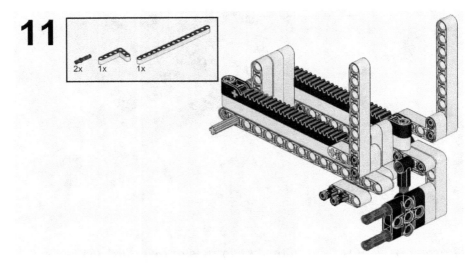

*Figure 8-11.* Slide on the last 3 × 5 beam, and then put on the 15M beam. Don't forget the 3M connector pegs

**12**

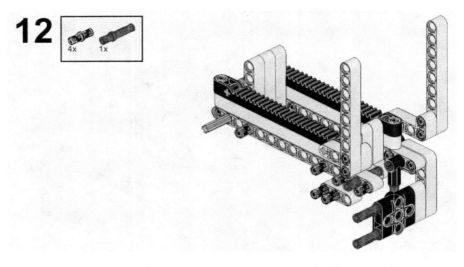

*Figure 8-12.* Put on the 3M connector pegs and other sized connector pegs

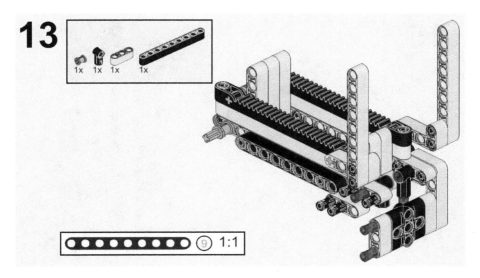

*Figure 8-13.* *Put on the #1 angle connector, put on the 9M and 3M beams, and then put on the bush on top*

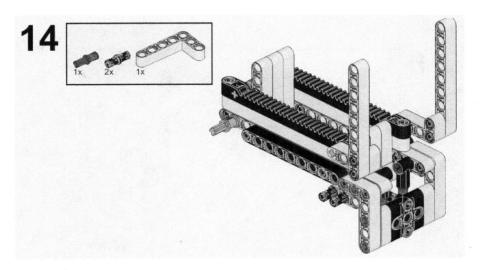

*Figure 8-14.* *Put on the two connector pegs and the 3 × 5 beam. Don't forget the connector peg/cross axle*

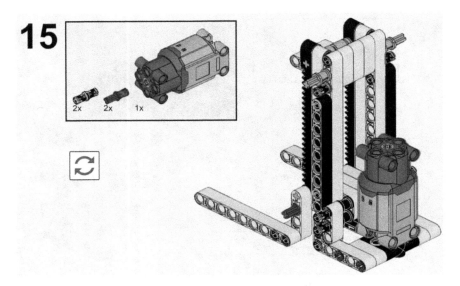

***Figure 8-15.*** *This step is pretty tricky, as it is time to put in the 9V motor, and it is time to put on the two connector pegs with cross axles and two connector pegs*

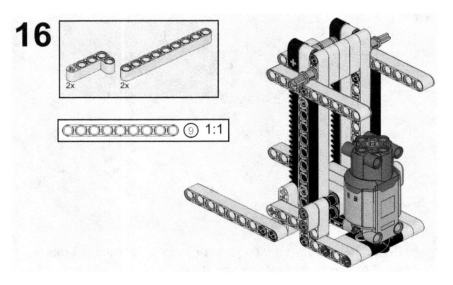

***Figure 8-16.*** *Put on the 9M and 2 × 4 beams*

**17**

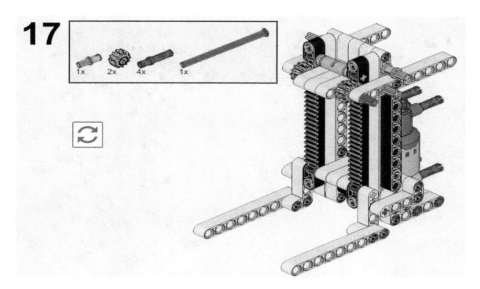

*Figure 8-17.* *Put on the 3M connector pegs on the 9V motor and the connector peg with cross axle (without friction). Put on the 8M axle with stop, and make certain that 12-tooth double bevel gear is meshed with the racks*

**18**

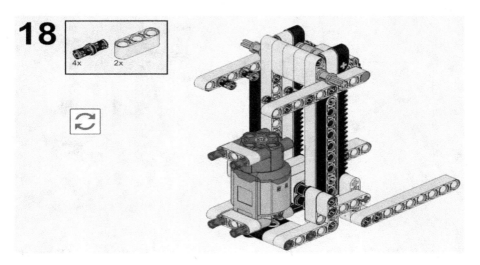

*Figure 8-18.* *Put on the 3M beams on the 3M connector pegs, and put on the four connector pegs above*

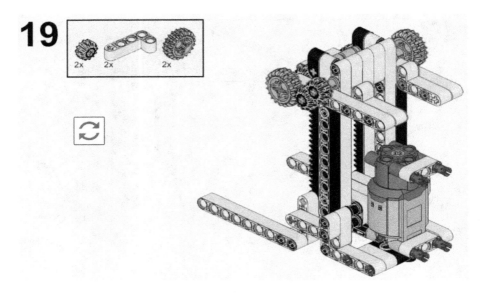

***Figure 8-19.*** *Put on the 2 × 4 beams, and put on the 12-tooth and 20-tooth double bevel gears so they mesh perfectly*

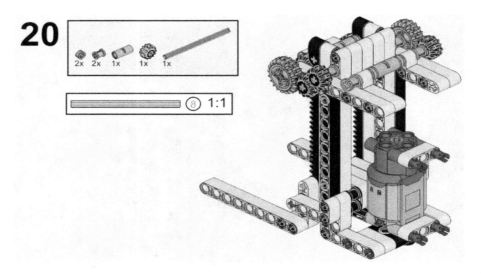

***Figure 8-20.*** *Use the half bushes, 2M tube, and bush, on the 8-tooth double bevel gear on the 8M axle*

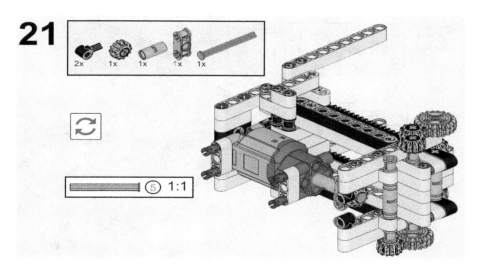

*Figure 8-21.* Use the 5M axle with stop to put on the tube, double cross block, and 8-tooth double bevel gear on the motor. Don't forget to put on the axle and peg connectors as shown

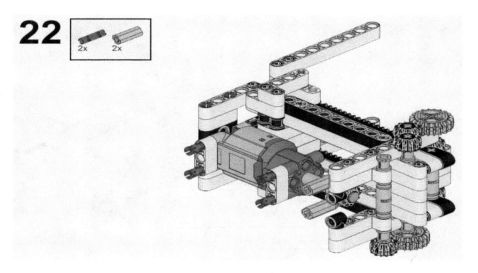

*Figure 8-22.* Put the 2M axles on the double cross block from the last step, and put on the Axle connectors

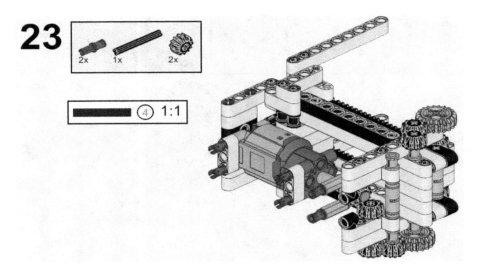

*Figure 8-23.* *Put on the connector peg/cross axles. Put on the 4M axle with the 8-tooth gear on each side as shown, meshed with the other gears*

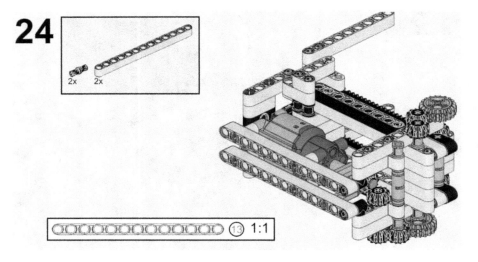

*Figure 8-24.* *Put on the connector pegs and the 13M beam*

All right, so you will notice that you can hook the 9V motor to the battery box, and you will see that the forks in the front will rise. It will jam up if it gets to the top, so don't let that happen for too long.

# Scissor Lift

If you have ever used a scissor lift in real life, there is something really great about how it can essentially raise something up and how it unfolds. I figured out a way to make that happen with Technic pieces, and it takes a smaller rack.

Please note that the motor used in this particular construction is one of the older types that isn't available any more from the LEGO website, but you can order it from other places like BrickLink. That, or figure out a way to use a newer motor. Please note that this, like the forklift, has no place to put a battery box. I will let you figure that out.

Now, this scissor lift will rise up pretty high, but I suppose that it could be made to rise up even higher. I say "suppose" because I didn't build it that way, and I don't think Stud.io could be programmed to show how successful you could be creating this. I will say that the amount it can lift seems pretty small.

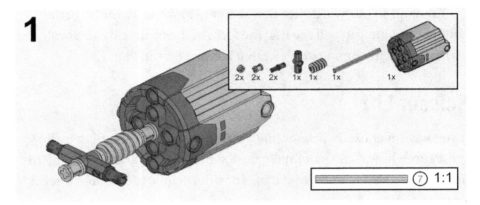

***Figure 8-25.*** *Start with the 9V motor XL, and slide on the 7M axle, the bush, a half bush, the worm gear, the half bush, and the #2 angle connector with connector peg/cross axles and with the bush*

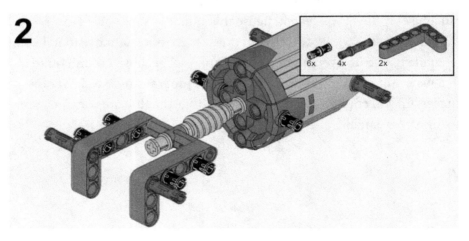

***Figure 8-26.*** *Put on the 3 × 5 beams, and put on the 3M connector pegs and other connector pegs as shown*

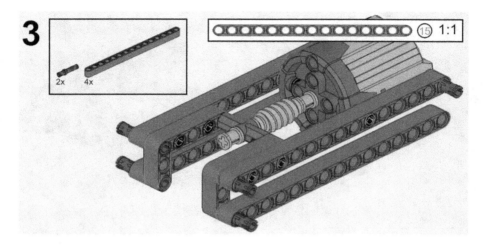

***Figure 8-27.*** *Put on the four 15M beams after putting on the 3M connector pegs*

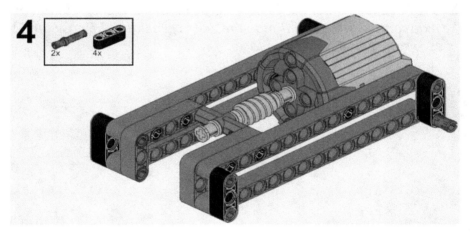

***Figure 8-28.*** *Put on the 3M connector pegs, and then put on the 3M beams as shown*

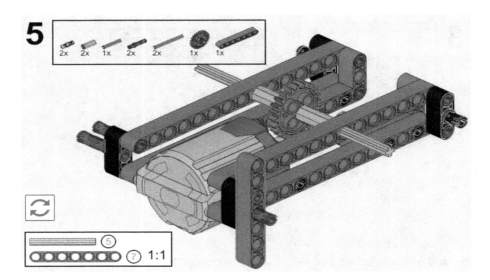

***Figure 8-29.*** *Put on the 3M connector pegs and connector pegs and then 7M beams. Center the 24-tooth gear on the 3M axle, and put on the axle connectors. Mesh that to the worm gear, and then use the 5M axles to secure that gear into place*

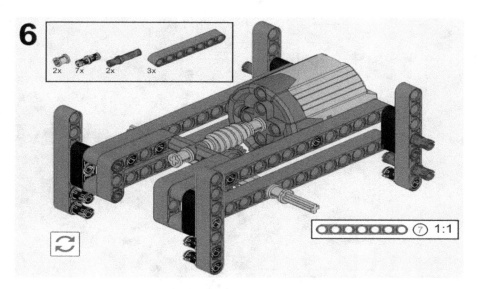

***Figure 8-30.*** *Put on the 7M beams, as well as the 3M connector pegs and other connector pegs. Put on the bushes as shown*

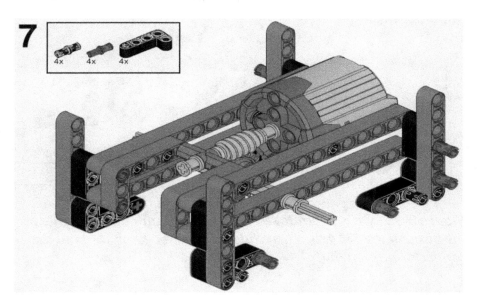

***Figure 8-31.*** *Put on the 2 × 4 beams, and then put on the connector peg/cross axles and connector pegs*

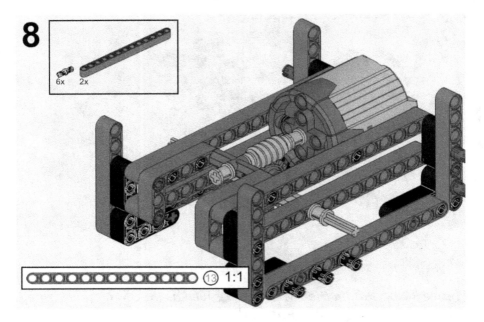

***Figure 8-32.*** *Put on the 13M beams, and then put on the connector pegs*

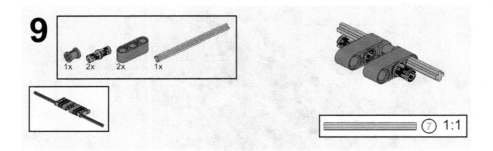

***Figure 8-33.*** *On a separate section from the main model, center the bush on the 7M axle. Then slide on the 3M beams, and put the connector pegs on that*

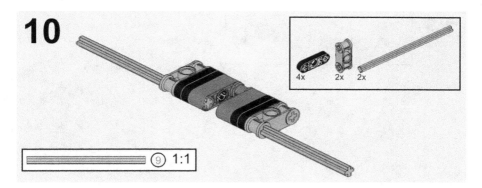

***Figure 8-34.*** *Put on the double cross blocks, as well as the 3M levers on each side and put on the 9M axles*

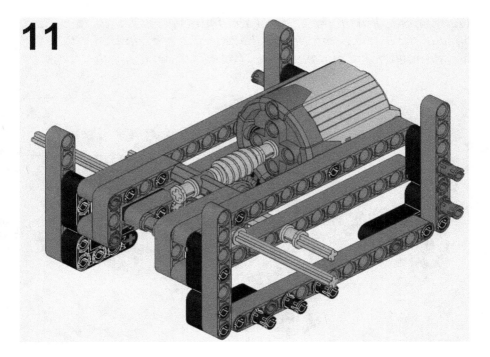

***Figure 8-35.*** *Put in the section from the last two sets as shown*

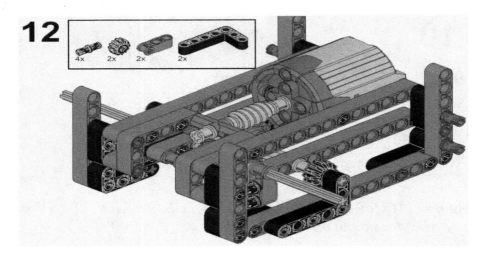

*Figure 8-36.* *Put on the 12-tooth double bevel gears and then cap it off with the 3 × 5 beams. Put on the axle and peg connector 3M with two through holes, and put in two connector pegs*

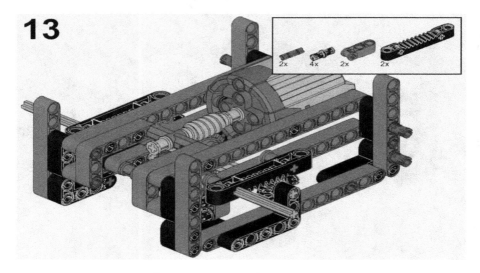

*Figure 8-37.* *Put on the 2M axle on the 7M gear rack, and then put on the axle and peg connector 3M with two through holes with connector pegs, and put that on the structure so the gears mesh perfectly with the racks*

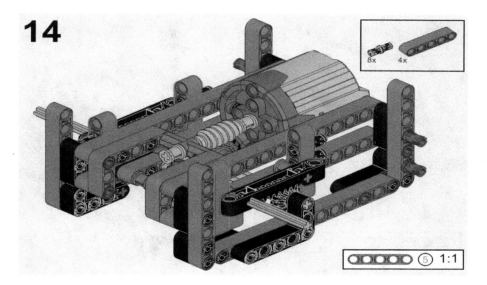

***Figure 8-38.*** *On the axle and peg connector 3M with two through holes, put on the 5M beams, and then put on the connector pegs*

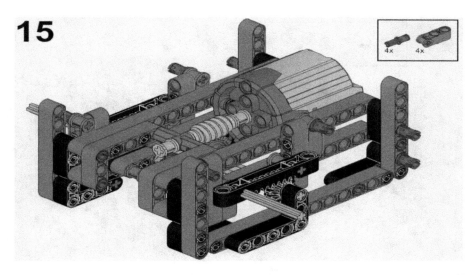

***Figure 8-39.*** *Put on the axle and connector peg 3M with two through holes, and put on the connector peg/cross axles on that*

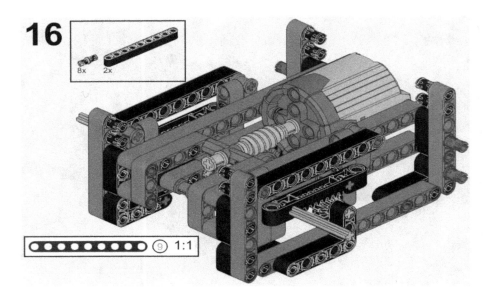

***Figure 8-40.*** *Put on the 9M beams, and then put on the eight connector pegs*

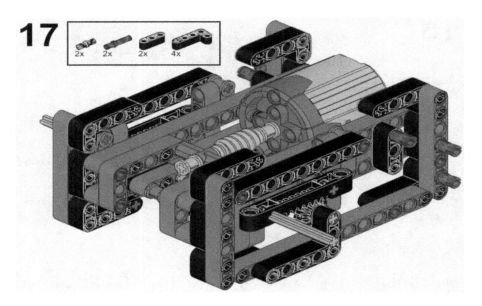

***Figure 8-41.*** *Put on the 3M connector pegs and other connector pegs and put a 3M beam on that, and then put on the 2 × 4 beams*

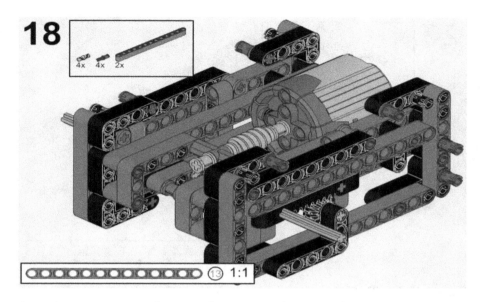

***Figure 8-42.*** *Put on the 13M beams, and put on the connector pegs and connector peg/cross axles*

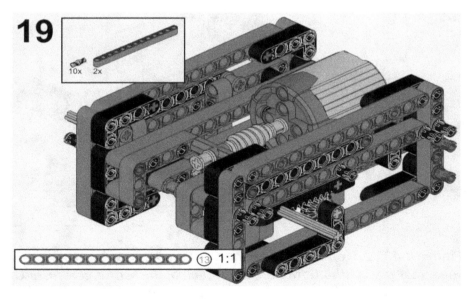

***Figure 8-43.*** *Put on the 13M beam, and put on the ten connector pegs*

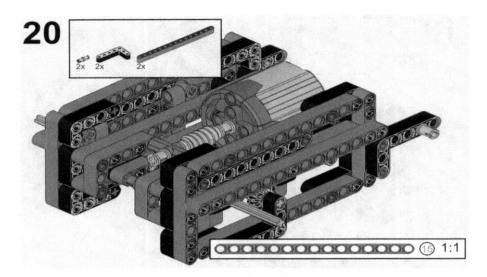

*Figure 8-44.* *Put on the 15M beam, and the 3 × 5 beams with a connector peg without friction*

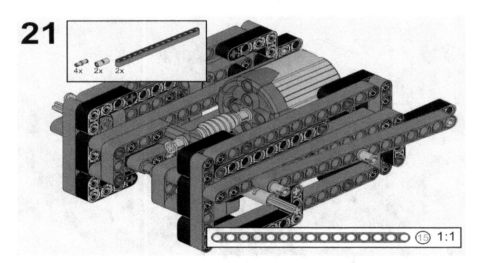

*Figure 8-45.* *Put on the 2M tube and put on the 15M beams with connector pegs without friction, and much of the beams get crossed at this point to form the lifting portion of the scissor lift*

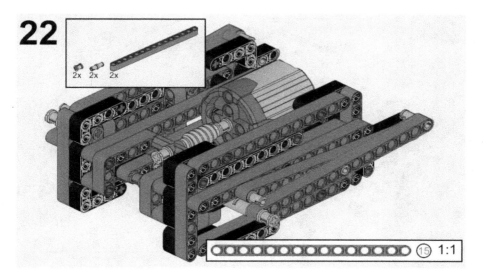

*Figure 8-46.* *Put on a 15M with the connector peg without friction, and put on the bush*

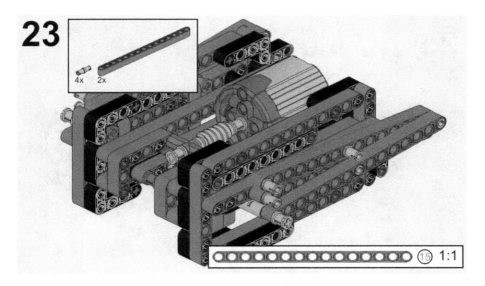

*Figure 8-47.* *Put on the 15M beam with the connector pegs without friction*

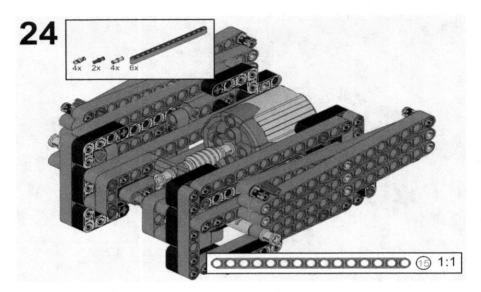

***Figure 8-48.*** *Put on the 15M beams with the connector pegs without friction, and put on the connector peg and connector peg/cross axles*

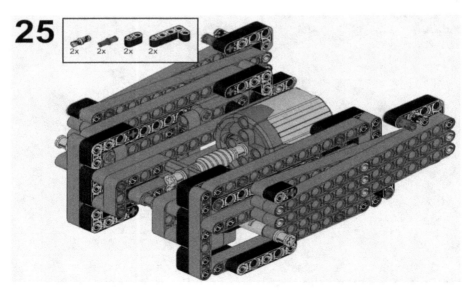

***Figure 8-49.*** *Put on the 2 × 4 beams with the connector pegs and connector pegs/cross axles, and then put on the 2M beam with cross axle*

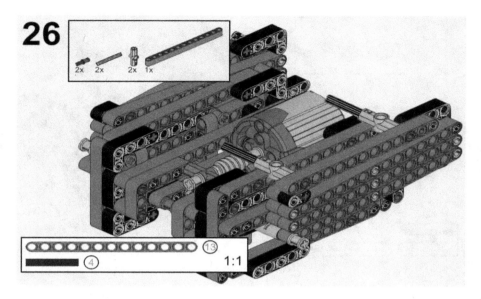

*Figure 8-50.* *Put on the 13M beam, and attach the connector peg/ cross axles and the #2 angle connectors, and put on the 4M axles*

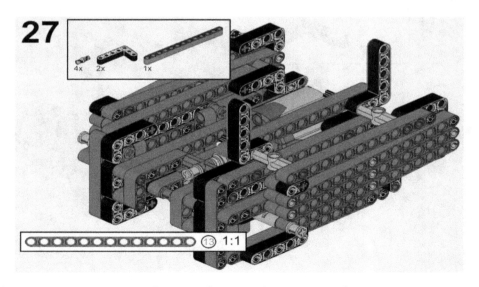

*Figure 8-51.* *Put on the 3 × 5 beams, then put on the connector pegs, and put on the 13M beam*

271

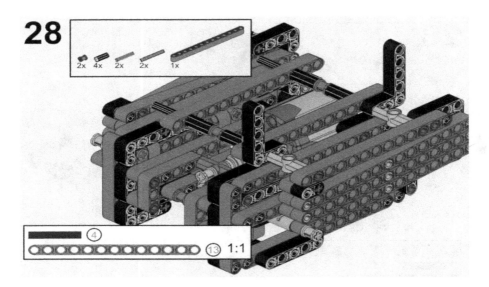

**Figure 8-52.** *Put on the axle connectors, 3M axles, bushes, axle connectors, 4M axles, and 13M beam*

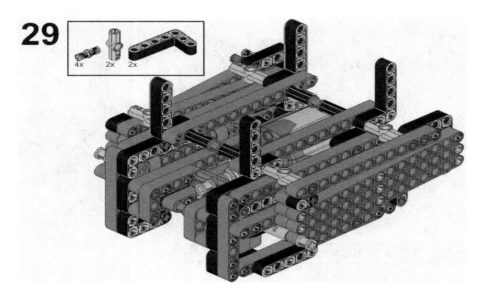

**Figure 8-53.** *Put on the connector pegs, with the two 3 × 5 beams and the #2 angle connectors*

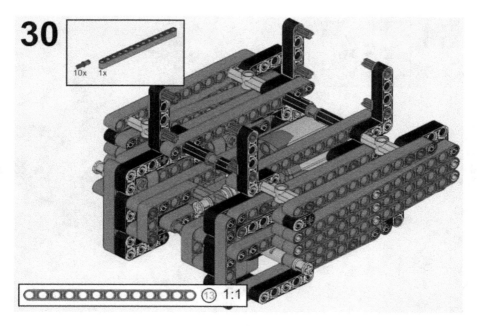

***Figure 8-54.*** *Put on the connector peg/cross axles on the #2 angle connectors, and then put on the 13M beam. Then put the other connector peg/cross axles on the 3 × 5 beams as shown*

**31**

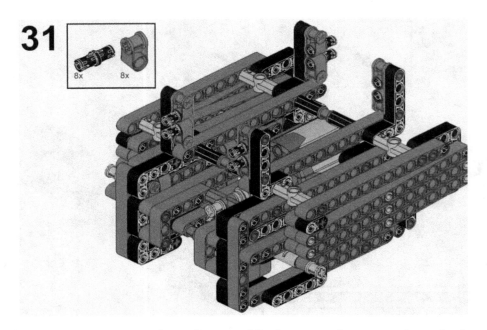

***Figure 8-55.*** *Put on the eight cross blocks on as shown, and put in the eight connector pegs*

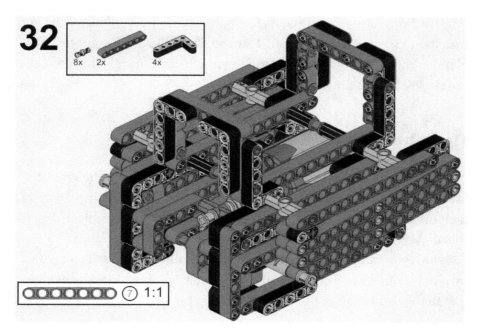

***Figure 8-56.*** *Put on the 3 × 5 beams, put on the connector pegs, and put on the 7M beams*

Once you have that all set up, just connect a battery to the motor, and turn it on to watch it rise and fall. Like the forklift, you will want to make certain that you do not raise the top too much, or let it sink down too low as this will jam up the gears.

# Conclusion

The best part of this construction equipment is it gives you the tools it takes to succeed to create more. You can see that a motorized gear and a rack can raise up a forklift, and something a little more complicated than that can create a scissorlift.

Now, you might be wondering: how can I make a crane that can turn on a swivel, like a real crane? Well, I'm going to go more into detail about that in this next chapter on LEGO Technic robots.

# CHAPTER 9

# LEGO Technic Robots

While LEGO Technic has been a very advanced way to create all kinds of vehicles with wheels, this is a chapter that is going to talk about another function: robots. I actually devoted an entire book to Technic robots, because I found that I really couldn't talk about them in a few chapters. Today, I am going to cram a lot of robot information into essentially one chapter of this book.

Actually, when it comes to robots, I have to admit that LEGO Technic is rather limited as far as what they can do. It was the LEGO MINDSTORMS kits that really went into a lot of detail as far as a LEGO robot could do. These kits had a CPU-style brick that you could program, and there were a lot of sensors made to detect color and other very advanced functions.

LEGO Technic is really all about creating remote controls which are very start and stop in their functionality. It really is all about creating something that can accommodate this type of functionality to create something that is rather robot-like.

## Our Fascination with Robots

The term of robot was first heard in a 1920 science fiction play called RUR (Rossum's Universal Robots) by Czech writer Karel Capek. While Karel Capek is often credited as the creator of this word, it was actually his brother, Josef Capek, who came up with the actual word itself, as Karel was having trouble coming up with a term for his beings of synthetic organic matter.

© Mark Rollins 2024
M. Rollins, *The Ultimate LEGO Technic Book*, Maker Innovations Series,
https://doi.org/10.1007/979-8-8688-0793-0_9

The play of RUR is about a race of robots and how they rose up against their human commanders. In many ways, this story was ahead of its time as robot uprisings are a typical convention of science fiction. By the way, it should be noted that the end of RUR has a scenario where the robots win, something that isn't in a lot of robot uprising stories.

Of course, it can be argued that one of the first robot stories was Mary Shelley's *Frankenstein* published almost a century before RUR in 1831, and there is a mechanical being in one of L. Frank Baum's Oz stories named Tik-Tok that predates RUR by a few decades. It's pretty obvious that RUR influenced Fritz Lang's *Metropolis*, which features a robot as a main character. Isaac Asimov, who wrote many science fiction stories about robots and developed the Three Laws, was not a fan of Capek's work, but admired its adding "robot" to the dictionary.

Even though we live in an age of AI, we are not really closer to bringing a robot in every home. Most of us have vacuum cleaners and other end user consumer electronics that are controllable and can reduce our labor workload, but it is not like we have some robotic servant that can help us when we really need it.

Of course, it feels like we are getting closer to that every day. Considering that we live in an AI age, it is not difficult to imagine someone giving an artificial body to an artificial mind. So maybe in the future we will have LEGO MINDSTORMS kits that will be able to create robotic beings that feel like C-3PO from *Star Wars* or even Data from *Star Trek: The Next Generation*, but for now, we have LEGO Technic for some remote control functionality.

# The Robot Walker

One of the things that I like about robots is how they can spark our imagination. It is not surprising that we are trying to create artificial people, as much of our technological inspirations stem from nature itself.

I'm guessing that we never would have conceived the airplane if we didn't have daily reminders that birds can fly, and we probably never would have even imagined a submarine if not for fish.

With that in mind, try to imagine what would have happened if the wheel were not invented and cars and other various vehicles worked with legs walking instead of tires rotating. These next set of instructions will show you how to create a Technic vehicle that can walk, but not only will it go one-dimensionally forwards and backwards, but it will turn as well.

## The Swivel

In the last chapter, I talked about how to make certain construction equipment and mentioned how cranes and other vehicles have swivels so the user can have better control. I feel it necessary to give an instruction on how to make a LEGO swivel, which is going to come into play in making our four-legged LEGO walker.

This particular swivel uses the turntable, and the trick is to make certain that it turns slowly. If you were to hook it up to gears from the motor itself, it spins like a tornado, but you need it to merely swerve slowly for steering functions.

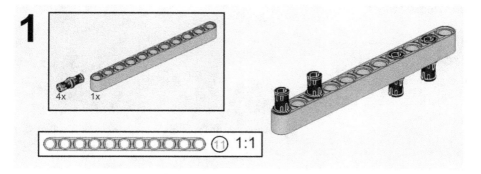

*Figure 9-1.* *Put the connector pegs in the 11M beam*

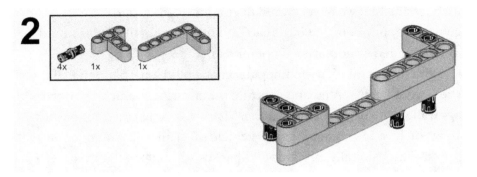

***Figure 9-2.*** *Put on the T-beam and 3 × 5 beam with the connector pegs*

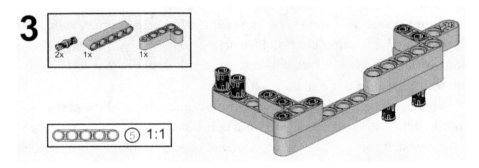

***Figure 9-3.*** *Put on the 5M beam with the 2 × 4 beam and connector pegs*

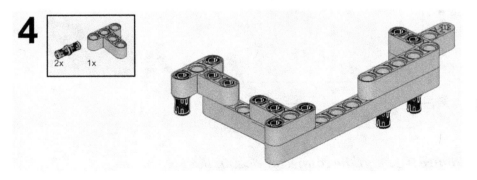

***Figure 9-4.*** *Put on the T-beam and the connector pegs*

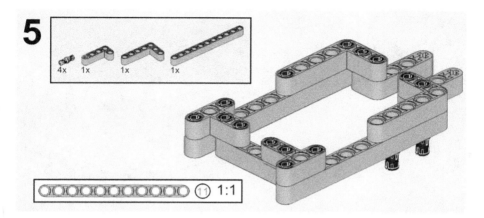

***Figure* 9-5.** *Put on the 3 × 5, 2 × 4, and 11M beams with the connector pegs*

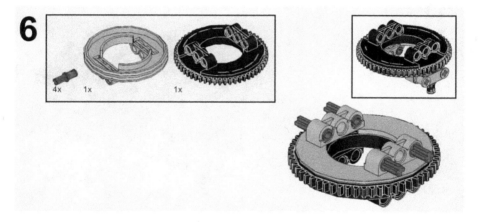

***Figure* 9-6.** *These turntable sections usually come as one piece, but this is how to put them together. Then put on the connector peg/ cross axles*

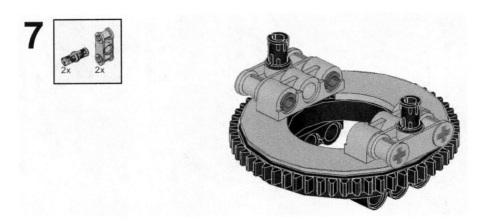

*Figure 9-7.* *Put on the cross blocks with the connector pegs*

*Figure 9-8.* *This is what it should like once the turntable section is complete, so flip it over*

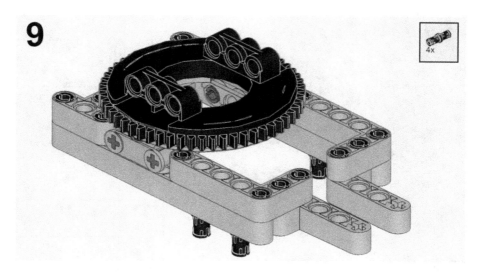

***Figure 9-9.*** *Connect the steps 6–8 to steps 1–5, and then add the connector pegs*

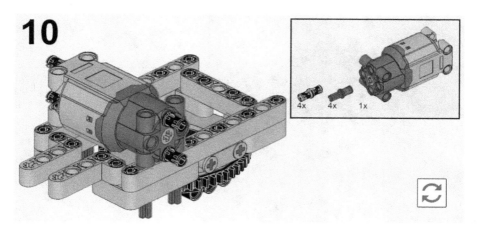

***Figure 9-10.*** *Put on the 9V Electric Motor with the connector peg and connector peg/cross axles*

**11**

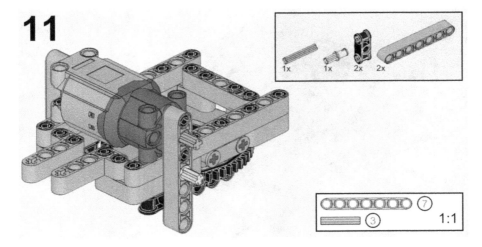

*Figure 9-11.* *Put on the cross blocks and the 7M beams, with the 3M axle and connector peg/cross axle with no friction*

**12**

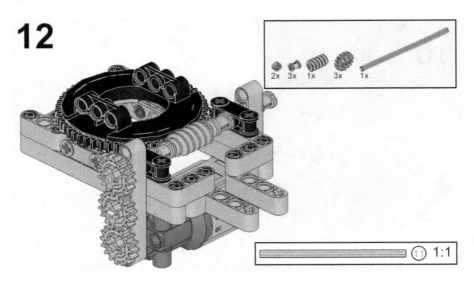

*Figure 9-12.* *Put on the 11M axle with the worm gear, half bushes, bushes, and then the 16-tooth gears*

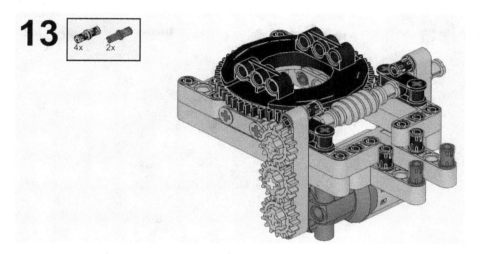

*Figure 9-13.* *Put on the connector peg and connector peg/cross axles*

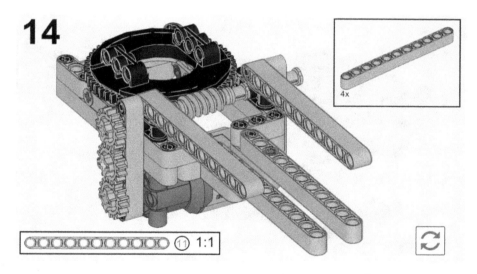

*Figure 9-14.* *Time to put on four 11M beams*

**15**

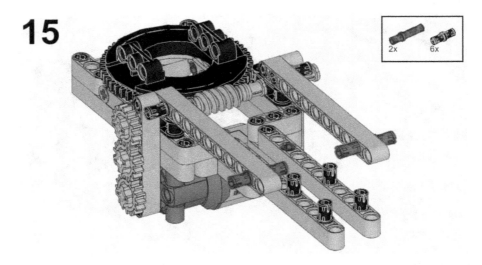

*Figure 9-15. Put on the 3M connector pegs and other connector pegs*

**16**

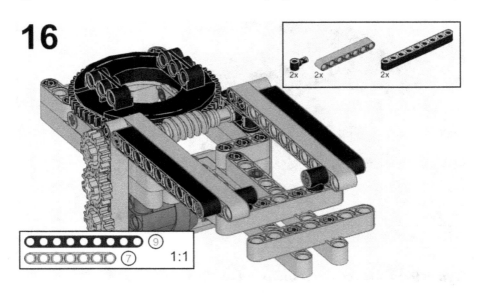

*Figure 9-16. Put on the 7M and 9M beams with the pin with holes*

**17**

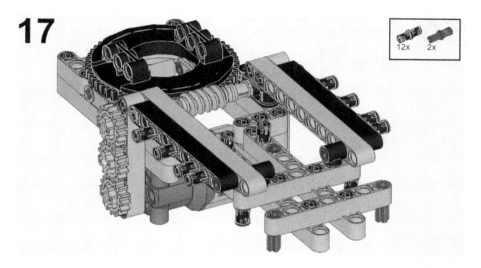

*Figure 9-17.* Put on the connector pegs and connector peg/cross axles

**18**

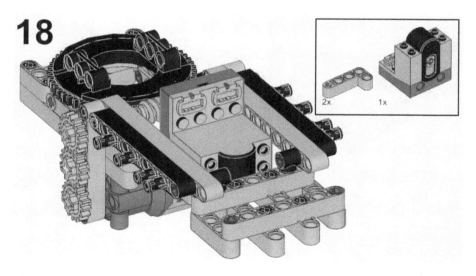

*Figure 9-18.* Put on the Electric Power Functions Receiver Unit and the 2 × 4 beams

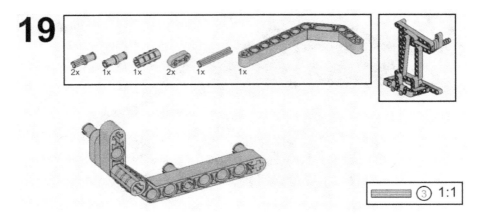

***Figure 9-19.*** *Use the 3M axle on the double bent beam with axle connector and 2M levers. Use connector peg and connector peg/cross axles (without friction)*

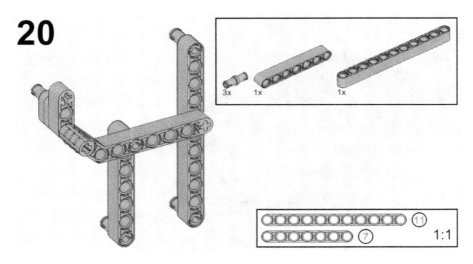

***Figure 9-20.*** *Time to put on the 7M and 11M beams, with the connector pegs (without friction)*

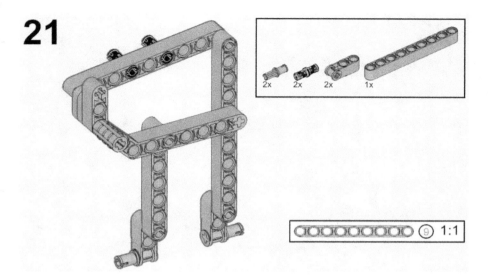

*Figure 9-21.* *Put on the 9M beam, the 3M cross blocks with axle, and the connector pegs and the connector peg/cross axles*

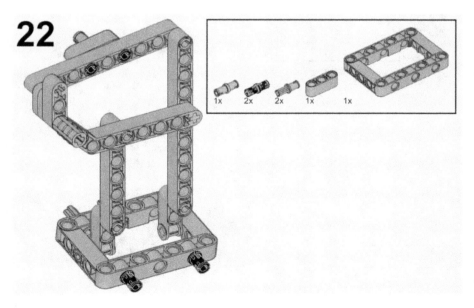

*Figure 9-22.* *Put on the 5 × 7 beam panel and the 3M beam. Then put on the connector pegs (with and without friction) and the connector peg/cross axles (without friction)*

**23**

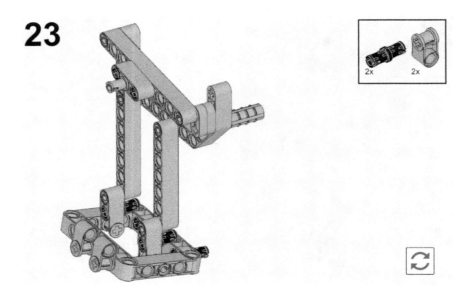

*Figure 9-23.* Put on the connector pegs and 90-degree cross blocks

**24**

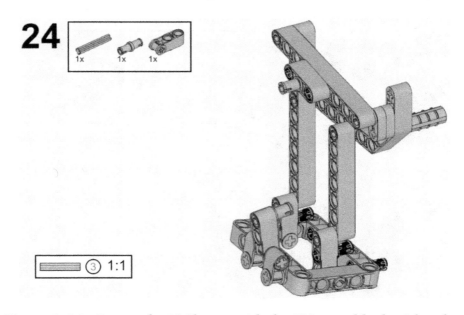

*Figure 9-24.* Put on the 3M beam with the 2M cross block with axle and the connector peg without friction

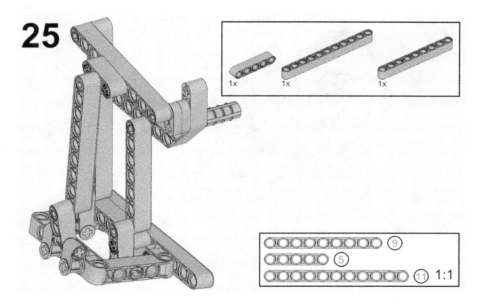

*Figure 9-25.* Put on the 5M, 9M, and 11M beams

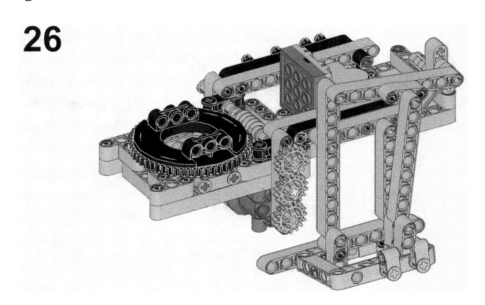

*Figure 9-26.* Put on the left leg as shown

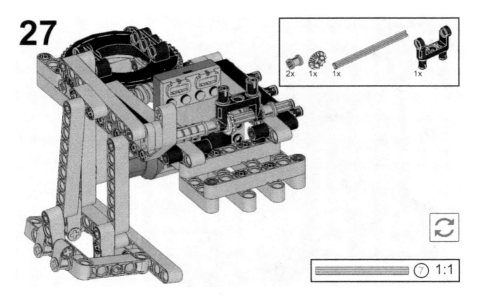

*Figure 9-27.* Use the 7M axle with the bushes, the 12-tooth bevel gear, and the pin connector toggle joint smooth double with two pins

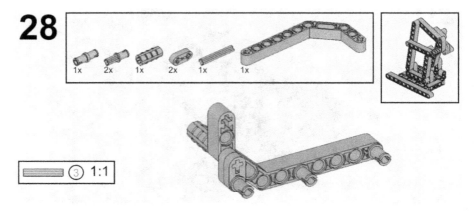

*Figure 9-28.* Use the 3M axle on the double bent beam with axle connector and 2M levers. Use connector peg and connector peg/cross axles (without friction)

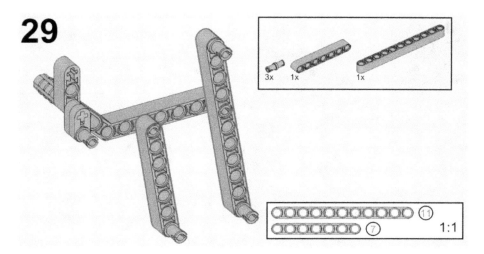

***Figure 9-29.*** *Time to put on the 7M and 11M beams, with the connector pegs (without friction)*

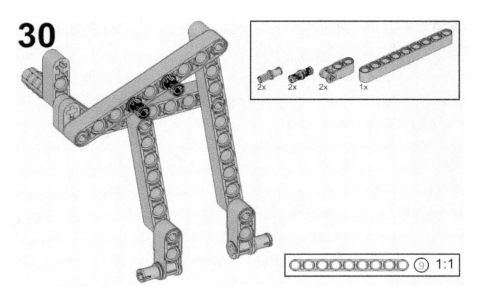

***Figure 9-30.*** *Put on the 9M beam, the 3M cross blocks with axle, and the connector pegs and the connector peg/cross axles*

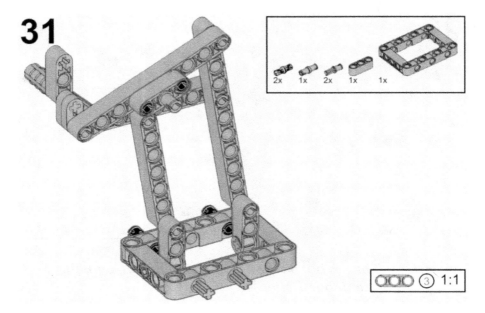

*Figure 9-31.* *Put on the 5 × 7 beam panel and the 3M beam. Put on the connector pegs (with and without friction) and connector peg/ cross axles (without friction)*

**32**

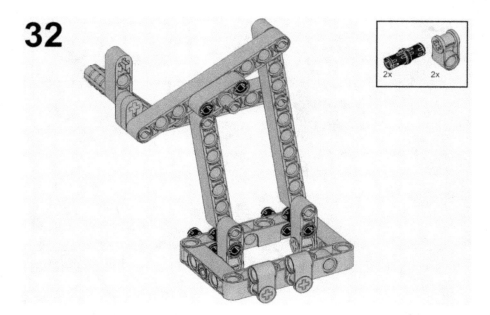

***Figure 9-32.*** *Put on the connector pegs and 90-degree cross blocks*

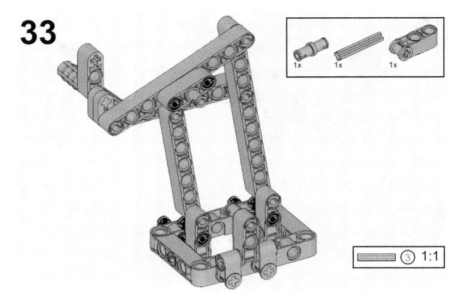

*Figure 9-33.* *Put on the 3M beam with the 2M cross block with axle and the connector peg without friction*

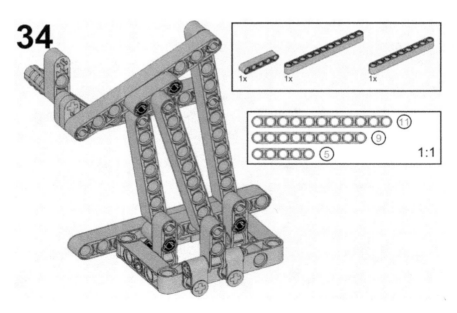

*Figure 9-34.* *Put on the 5M, 9M, and 11M beams*

**35**

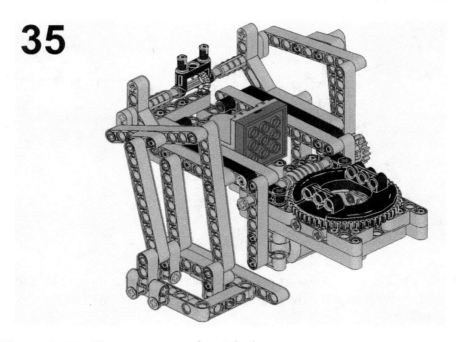

*Figure 9-35.* *Time to put on the right leg*

**36**

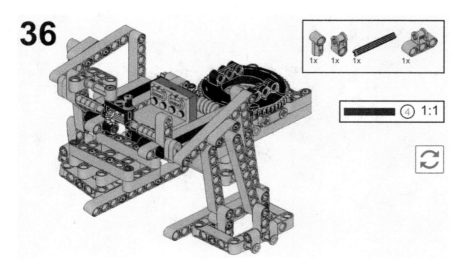

*Figure 9-36.* *Put on the #1 angle connector, the 90-degree cross block, and the axle and pin connector perpendicular triple, linked with the 4M axle*

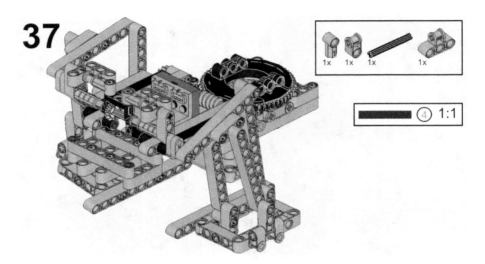

***Figure 9-37.*** *Put on the #1 angle connector, the 90-degree cross block, and the axle and pin connector perpendicular triple, linked with the 4M axle*

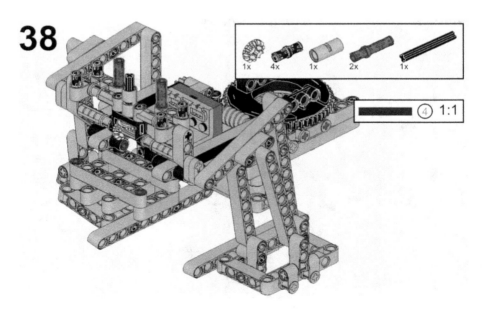

***Figure 9-38.*** *Put on the 4M axle, 2M tube, 3M connector pegs, connector pegs, and the 12-tooth gear bevel*

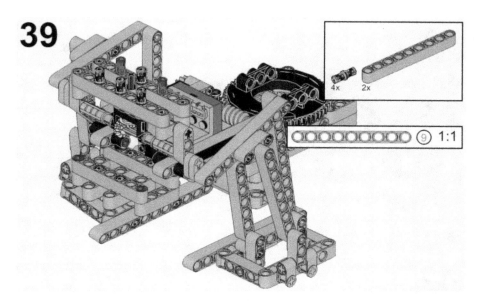

*Figure 9-39.* *Put on the 9M beams and the connector pegs*

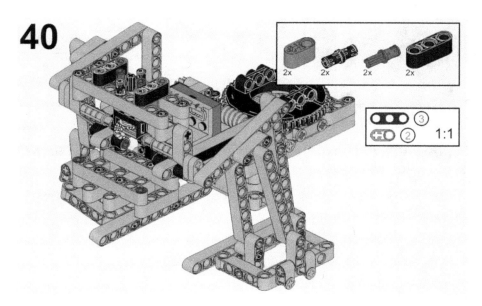

*Figure 9-40.* *Put on the connector pegs, the connector peg/cross axles, the 3M beams, and the 2M beam with cross axle*

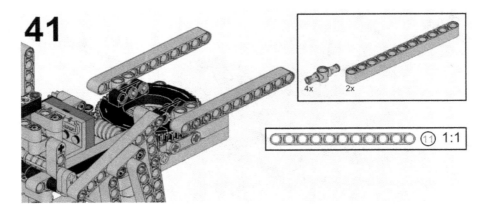

*Figure 9-41.* Put on the 3M pin with center pin hole and 11M beams

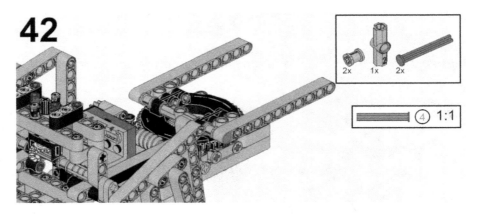

*Figure 9-42.* Put on the 4M axles with stops, the bushes, and the #1 angle connector

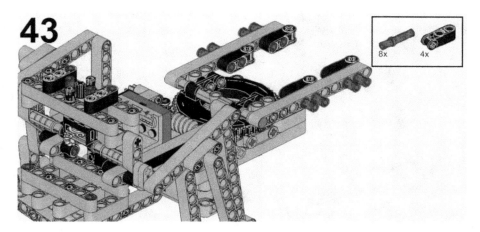

*Figure 9-43.* Put on the 3M connector pegs with the 3M cross blocks with axle hole

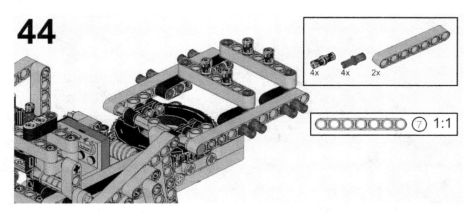

*Figure 9-44.* Put on the 7M beams and the connector pegs with connector peg/cross axles

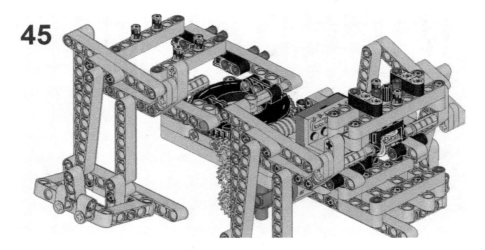

**Figure 9-45.**  *Repeat steps 19–25, and put on the left leg*

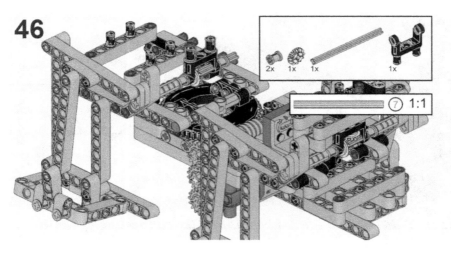

**Figure 9-46.**  *Use the 7M axle with the bushes, the 12-tooth bevel gear, and the pin connector toggle joint smooth double with two pins*

***Figure 9-47.*** *Repeat steps 28–34 and put on the right leg*

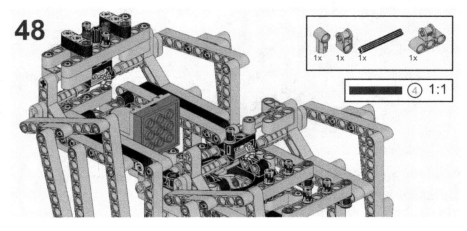

***Figure 9-48.*** *Put on the #1 angle connector, the 90-degree cross block, and the axle and pin connector perpendicular triple, linked with the 4M axle*

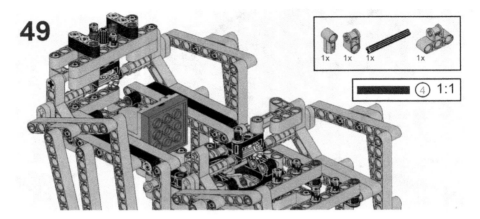

*Figure 9-49.* *Put on the #1 angle connector, the 90-degree cross block, and the axle and pin connector perpendicular triple, linked with the 4M axle*

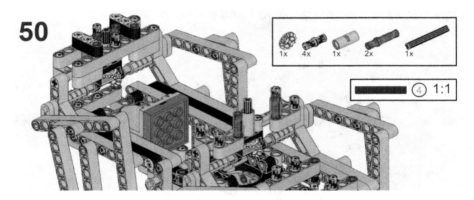

*Figure 9-50.* *Put on the 4M axle, 2M tube, 3M connector pegs, connector pegs, and the 12-tooth gear bevel*

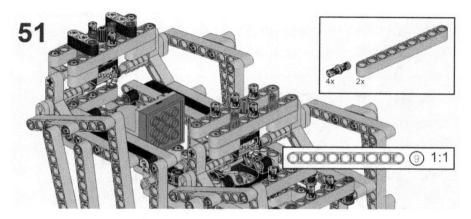

***Figure 9-51.*** *Put on the 9M beams and the connector pegs*

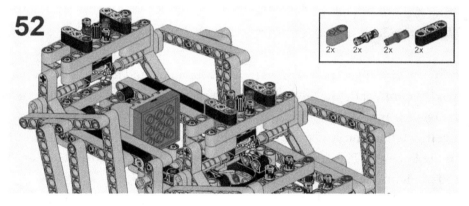

***Figure 9-52.*** *Put on the connector pegs, the connector peg/cross axles, the 3M beams, and the 2M beam with cross axle*

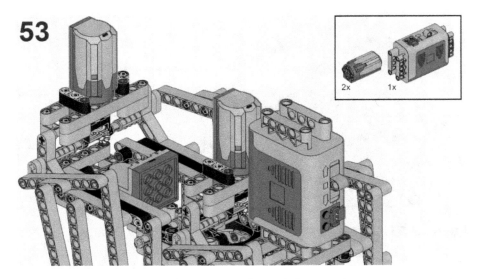

**53**

2x    1x

*Figure 9-53. Put on the battery pack and the two 9V motors*

Okay, if you got this far, then here is what you need to do. You will need to connect the Receiver to the battery box. Then you will need to take the wires from the two engines from the last step and stick the two ends together where the studs and metal join. Then attach that to the blue port on the Receiver. Then take the wire from the engine below the Receiver and put it on the blue port on the Receiver.

From there, sync whatever remote that you are using, and you will discover that the robot walker can walk forwards and backwards. I admit that I had some difficulty with this when it was steering, but the swivel does work, but occasionally, repeated walking will cause the legs to kind of veer off course.

I am going to readily admit that this model isn't exactly perfect, and if you can find a way to improve upon it, I would do it. Maybe you can figure out a way to make it go up a flight of stairs.

Before I end the chapter, I wanted to discuss something that I stated in the last chapter when talking about construction equipment. The swivel that is in steps 1–12 can be used on something like a crane, as it can provide a swivel motion. Proper application of the swivel can be used to make a raising motion as well, sort of like how your arm can swivel as well. I will leave it up to you to figure out how to build that.

# Conclusion

In discussing how to make LEGO Technic walk, it really is a matter of not only making the robot legs, but creating a proper mechanism to make certain that they step properly. Once you have that, you can take control using a remote and make what you like walk forward or backward.

However, you don't want just one-dimensional motion, do you? Of course not! That's why you can use the application of the swivel, which can do so many things, in order to create a way to make your walking robot turn. Once again, it is important to figure out how do that as well.

With all of this from the last few chapters, we are definitely gearing up for a finale.

# CHAPTER 10

# Final Thoughts

All right, I've had a great time creating with LEGO Technic, and I want to say a few final words about the experience. Much of this has been about building something like a car, plane, helicopter, or something that already exists. What I want to talk about is building something that is really "out of the box," and I don't mean a LEGO box, but something that really works with LEGO Technic.

Once you finish this book, I really want you to be able to sit down and create your own LEGO Technic mechanical creations. I honestly believe that you can use LEGO Technic to create anything, provided you have unlimited access to LEGO Technic pieces. Yes, you can create a lot of programmable machines with LEGO MINDSTORMS, but those are unfortunately not on the market anymore (not that you can't buy the specialized pieces on BrickLink, eBay, or other online auction services).

If you really think about it, most of the machines that we use on a daily basis, like our car and smartphone, are very complex, and we generally don't give them a second thought unless they break down on us. I've always admired inventors like the Wright brothers or Thomas Alva Edison for being pioneers into the world of technology, because they believed that machines could make our work easier, and there is a lot we can do that is easier because of machines.

So what I'm saying is that it is your turn now, and you get to figure out how to create something that is really going to be automated.

© Mark Rollins 2024
M. Rollins, *The Ultimate LEGO Technic Book*, Maker Innovations Series,
https://doi.org/10.1007/979-8-8688-0793-0_10

# My Random Project

For me, I am often fascinated by projects that I see online, and as I have mentioned before, there are many YouTube channels devoted to LEGO. Whenever I see a LEGO Technic project that looks very awesome, the only thing that I can think of is: "Oh, I want to build that." Then, when you try to build it, you run into a problem of figuring out how the builder got it to work.

For example, I once saw this video of a LEGO project that had a swimming fish, which was made with traditional LEGO bricks, but it was motorized and had a tail that moved like a real fish. It definitely fascinated me, and I knew that I had make one of my own in LEGO Technic.

So I got to work, trying to figure out how to make a fish body that moved like one. I decided on hooking up two gears together and then finding a way to connect to sections of a fish to them so they would essentially move up and down like a fish.

At first, I had it hooked up so the fish body would move side to side, but then I suddenly realized that if I was going to do a fish, I might as well do a fish that would look like a fish that I wanted to see. The swimming fish that I was trying to imitate in LEGO Technic was originally orange, but I have very few orange LEGO Technic bricks. I did have a lot of black and white LEGO Technic bricks, so I decided to make a killer whale or orca, because my wife really likes those.

I then did the research and discovered that an Orca whale has a tail that swishes up and down and not side to side, so I just decided to turn the model sideways. Sometimes fixing a problem in a LEGO Technic creation is just that simple, but I will have to say that most of the time, it is very complex, occasionally requiring a full rebuild to fix a simple problem.

Anyway, if you are interested in seeing the creation of the mechanized orca, here are the instructions.

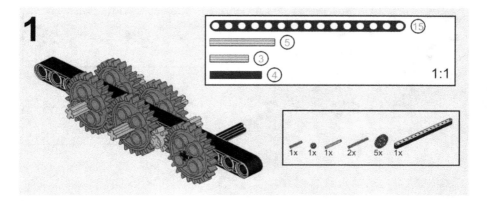

**Figure 10-1.** *Use the 3M, 4M, and 5M axles to put on the 24-tooth and 8-tooth gears on the 15M beam*

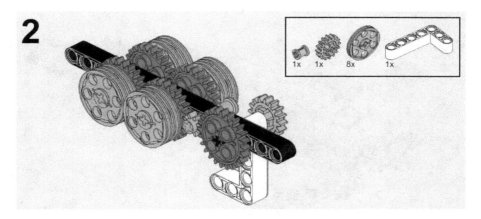

**Figure 10-2.** *Put on the bush and the 16-tooth gear at the end of the axles, but don't forget the 3 × 5 beam. Then put on the two wedge belt wheel pullies on each side of the 5M axles*

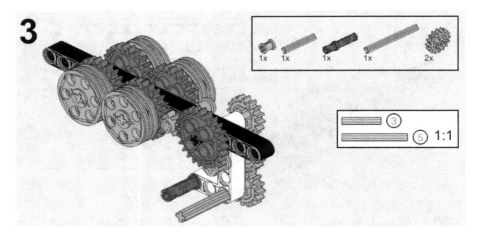

**Figure 10-3.** *Put on the 5M and 3M axles with the 16-tooth gears and the 3M connector peg. Be certain all the gears mesh together*

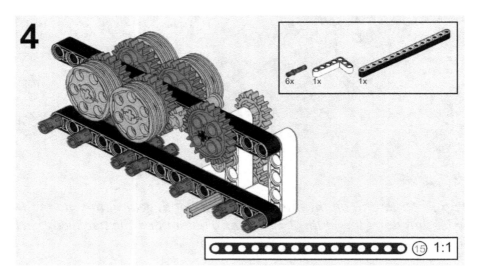

**Figure 10-4.** *Put on the 15M beam as shown, as well as the 3 × 5 beam. Also put on the 3M connector pegs*

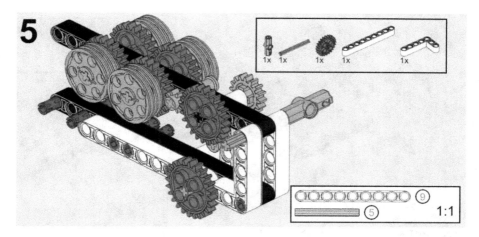

***Figure 10-5.*** *Put on the 3 × 5 and 9M beam, and the 24-tooth gear Then use the #2 angle connector with 5M axle*

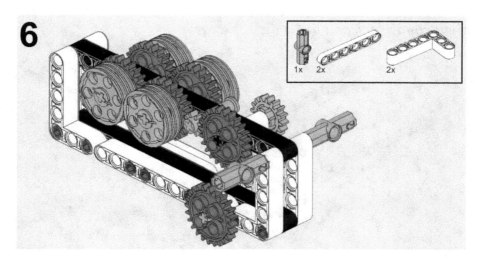

***Figure 10-6.*** *Put on the two 3 × 5 beams on the end, and put on the two 6M levers. Add on the #2 angle connector on top*

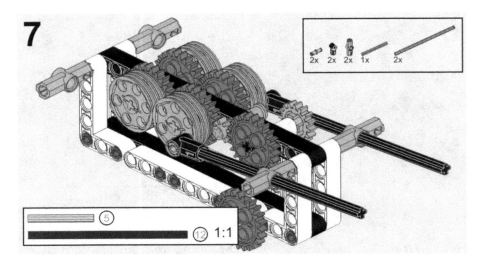

**Figure 10-7.** *Put on the 5M axle and the two #2 angle connectors. Put on the connector pegs without friction on, and then put on the #1 angle connectors, and insert the 12M axles*

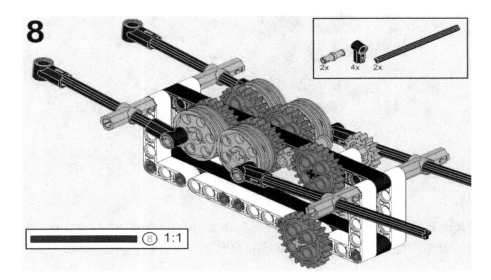

**Figure 10-8.** *Put on the connector pegs without friction on, and then put on the #1 angle connectors, and insert the 8M axles*

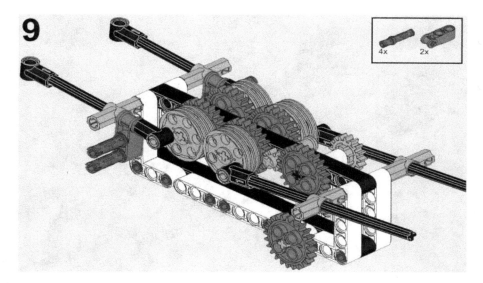

***Figure 10-9.*** *Put on the 3M cross block with axle hole, and then insert the 3M connector pegs*

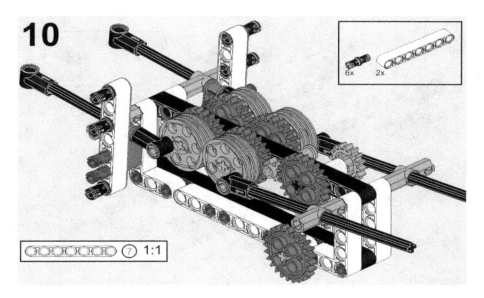

***Figure 10-10.*** *Put on the 7M beams with the connector pegs as shown*

315

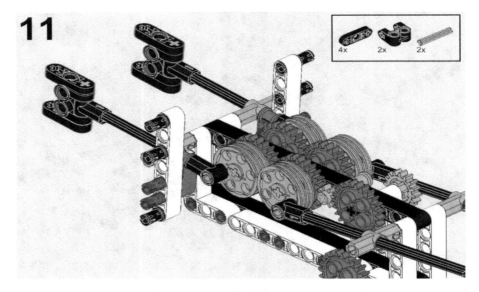

***Figure 10-11.*** *Put on the axle and connector peg with perpendicular double split, and then put on the 3M axles and the 3M levers as shown*

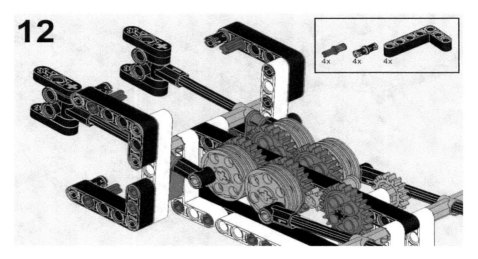

***Figure 10-12.*** *Put on the 3 × 5 beams with the connector pegs and connector peg/cross axles*

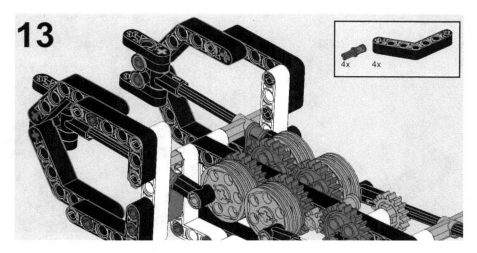

*Figure 10-13.* Put on the four 4 × 4 beams with the four connector peg/cross axles

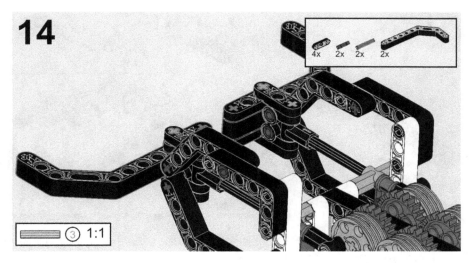

*Figure 10-14.* Put on the two double angle beams, and put on the 3M beams with the 2M and 3M axles

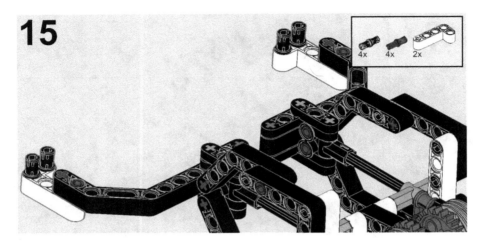

*Figure 10-15.* *Put on the connector peg/cross axles, then the 2 × 4 beams, and then the four connector pegs*

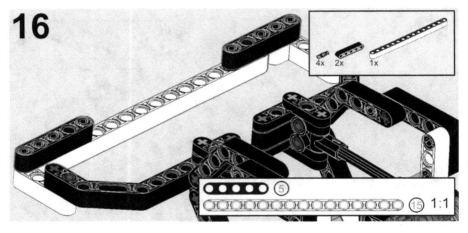

*Figure 10-16.* *Put on the 5M beam with the connector pegs, and then bridge them with the 15M beam*

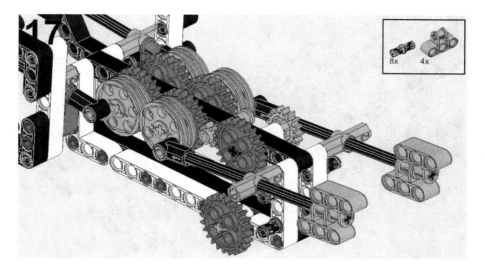

***Figure 10-17.*** *Put on the connector pegs as shown, and then slide on the axle and peg connector perpendicular triple*

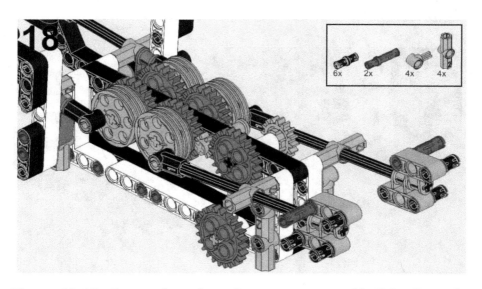

***Figure 10-18.*** *Put on the axle and peg connector with 1M axle, and put on the two #2 angle connectors. Then put on the regular and 3M connector pegs*

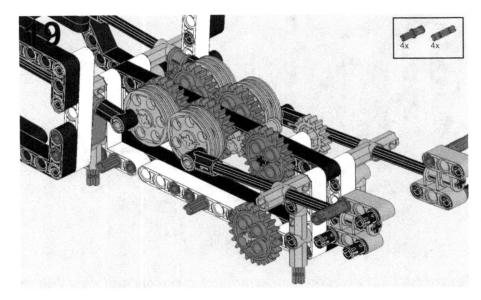

**Figure 10-19.** *Put on the connector peg/cross axles, and then put on the 2M axles below*

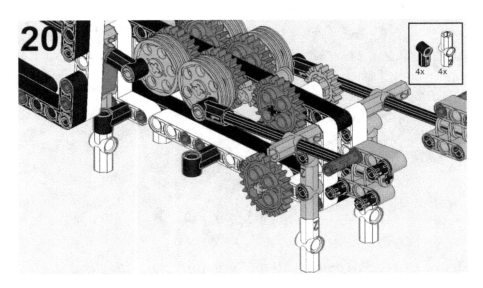

**Figure 10-20.** *Put on the #1 angle connectors, and then insert the four #2 angle connectors*

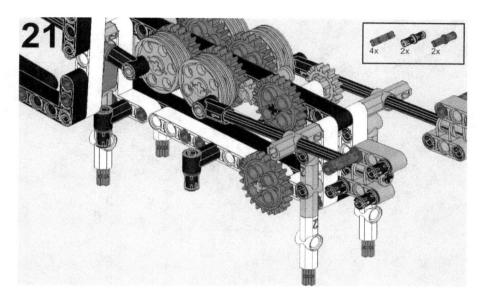

***Figure 10-21.*** *Put on the 2M axles, the connector pegs, and the connector peg/cross axles*

***Figure 10-22.*** *Put on the 9V motor, as well as the six #2 angle connectors*

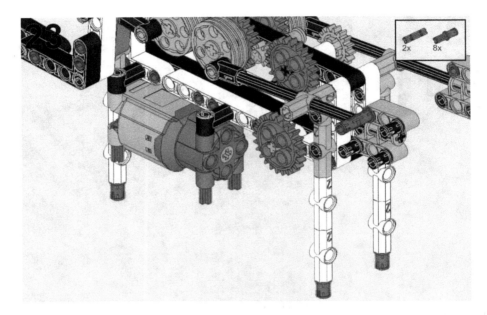

***Figure 10-23.*** *Put on the 2M axles, as well as the connector peg/ cross axles*

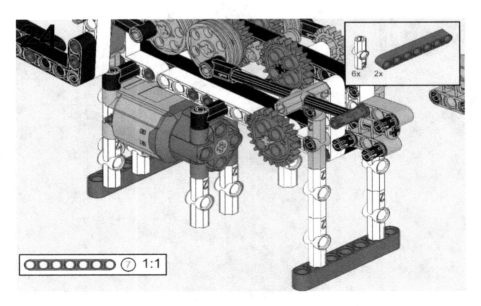

***Figure 10-24.*** *Put on the #2 angle connectors and then the 7M beams*

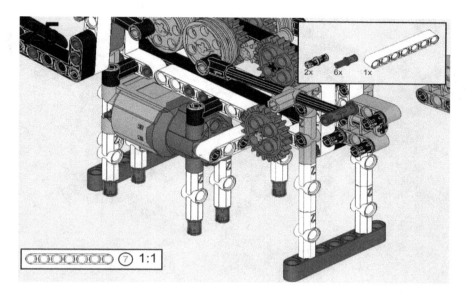

**Figure 10-25.** *Put on the connector pegs and the 7M beam. Put the connector pegs/cross axles on the bottom*

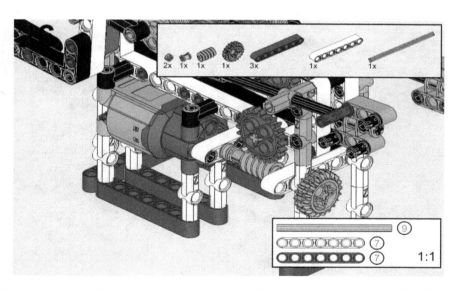

**Figure 10-26.** *Put on 7M beam on the bottom. Put on the 9M axle with the half bushes, bush, 7M beam, and the worm gear with the 20-tooth double bevel gear*

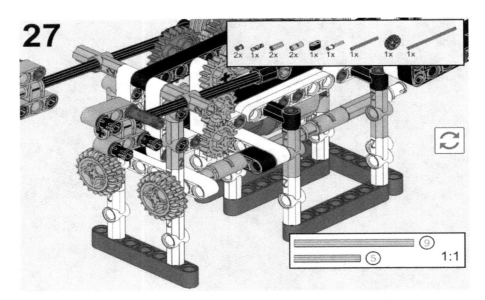

*Figure 10-27.*  *Put on the 5M and 9M axles with the axle connectors, bushes, and tube, with the 2M beam with axle hole*

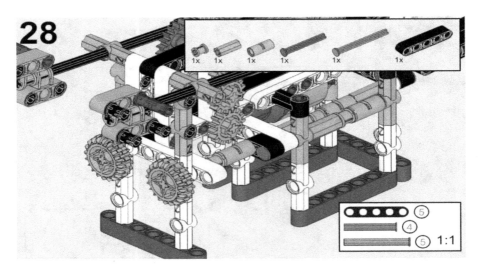

*Figure 10-28.*  *Put on 4M and 5M axles with stops, and use the axle connector, tube, and bush. Put on the 5M beam*

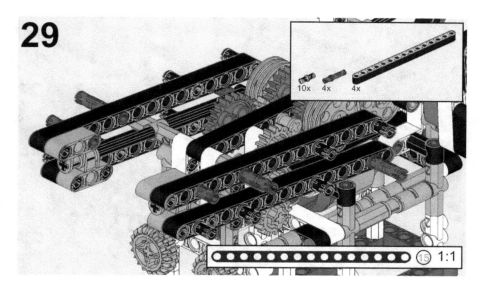

*Figure 10-29.* Put on the 15M beam, and put on the connector pegs with 3M connector pegs

*Figure 10-30.* Put on the 7M beams with the connector peg/ cross axles

*Figure 10-31.* *Put on the 13M beams and the connector pegs*

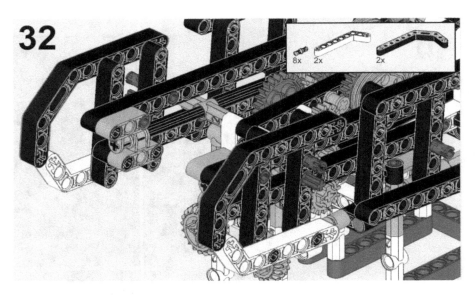

*Figure 10-32.* *Put on the double angle beams and the 1 × 7 beams, along with the connector pegs*

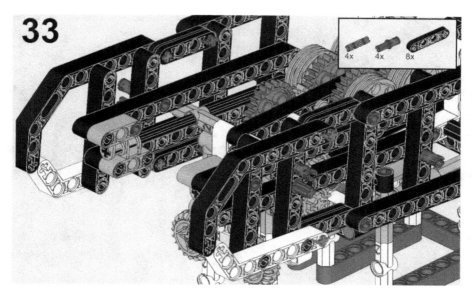

*Figure 10-33.* Put on the connector peg/cross axles and the 2M axles, and then put on the 4M levers

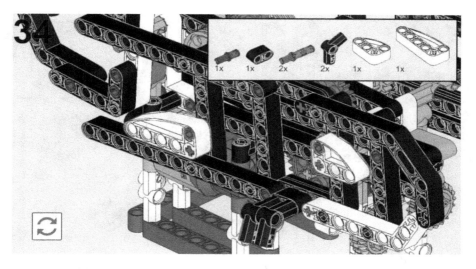

*Figure 10-34.* Put on the L-shape quarter ellipse 2 × 3 and the L-shape quarter ellipse 2 × 5. Put on the axle with 2M connector peg, the #5 angle connector, the 2M beam with axle hole, and connector peg/cross axles

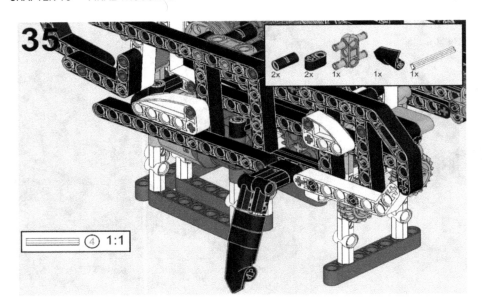

***Figure 10-35.*** *Put on the connector peg perpendicular with tubes. Put on the 4M axle, the 2M beams with axle holes, and the #8 panel*

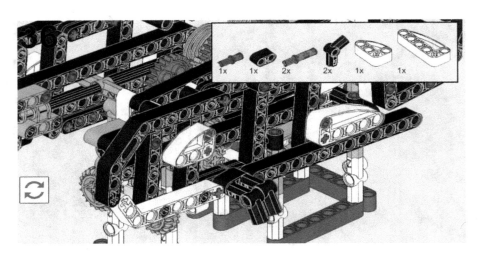

***Figure 10-36.*** *Put on the L-shape quarter ellipse 2 × 3 and the L-shape quarter ellipse 2 × 5. Put on the axle with 2M connector peg, the #5 angle connector, the 2M beam with axle hole, and connector peg/cross axles*

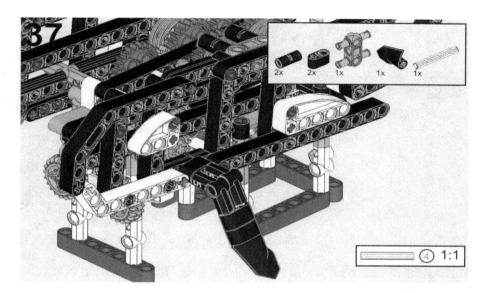

**Figure 10-37.** *Put on the connector peg perpendicular with tubes. Put on the 4M axle, the 2M beams with axle holes, and the #8 panel*

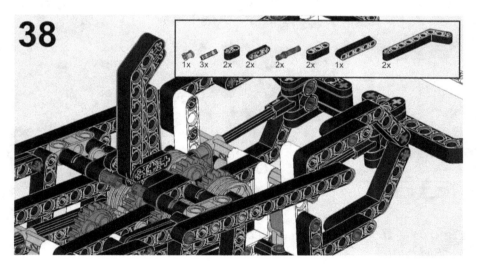

**Figure 10-38.** *Put on the 2M beams with axle hole, the 3M beams, the 5M beam, and the 2 × 7 beams for the tail fin*

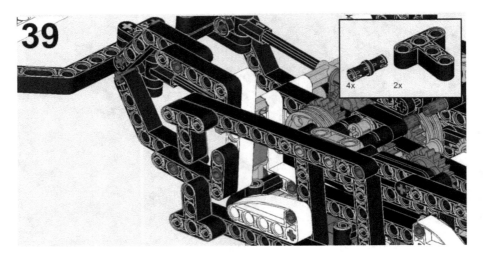

***Figure 10-39.*** *Insert the four connector pegs, followed by the two T-beams*

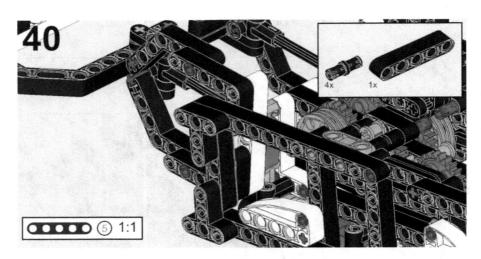

***Figure 10-40.*** *Put on the connector pegs, and then bridge them with the 5M beam*

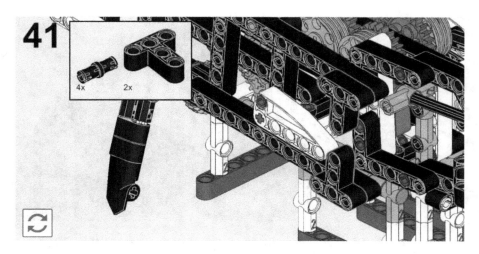

**Figure 10-41.** *Insert the four connector pegs, followed by the two T-beams*

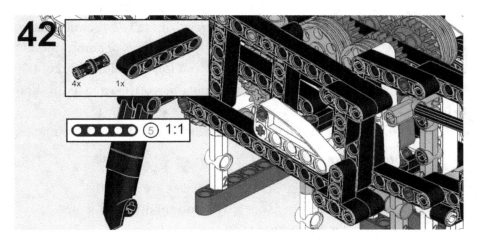

**Figure 10-42.** *Put on the connector pegs, and then bridge them with the 5M beam*

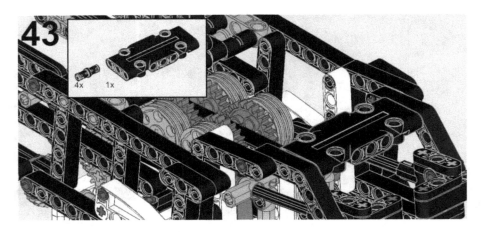

***Figure 10-43.*** *Put on the connector pegs, and then put the panel plate 3 × 7 × 1 in between*

All right, now that I have completed my last set of instructions, I want to encourage you to figure out what to do next with LEGO Technic. Maybe you want to create a model of a car, helicopter, airplane, or some kind of machine the LEGO currently doesn't have a kit for. I absolutely encourage you to do that, and you can use any principle that you learned in this book to help you.

I want to leave you with ten points on working with LEGO Technic.

1)   Organize your pieces.

I said before that LEGO Technic pieces are limited, in the sense that there are fewer kinds of them compared to traditional LEGO bricks. However, I would recommend taking the time to organize what you have if you haven't already.

After all, you don't want to be in the middle of a project and find that you can't proceed unless you have this very specific part. That has happened to me on many occasions, and it is just easier to purchase some tackleboxes or other types of organizers that will put your LEGO Technic pieces within an arm's reach.

2) Learn some mechanics.

You might have noticed that several creations in this book are based on real-world mechanical principles. For example, many cars use rack-in-pinion steering, and LEGO cars can use those as well.

You don't have to become a mechanical expert to see that gears and axles are part of everyday machinery, so it just makes sense that they integrate in LEGO Technic, and they can be used for some great building projects.

So the next time you see something that looks complex and mechanical, and you want to replicate it in LEGO Technic, find the time to take a closer look at it. Maybe you will be able to learn how it works and how easy it can translate into LEGO Technic.

3) Build strong.

When I was writing my other book about LEGO Worldbuilding, I discussed the "two-stud overlap" rule which is a way of creating a very secure bind by overlapping two pieces with two studs involved.

I highly recommend using as many connector pegs to hold beams together as needed, oversecuring if this is possible. When it comes to complex structures, where gears have to turn and mesh precisely, this is where the structure around them has to be tight.

So yes, make certain that what you build can't be easily ripped apart, even if it means that you might have to rebuild your project again to make certain that it works more efficiently.

4) If it is motorized, make sure you can put in the motor (and battery).

One of the most difficult things in building with LEGO Technic is to get your contraption working. Then it gets really complicated when you need to add a motor and a battery to power it.

My advice is that you take advantage of the large spaces in your model itself in order to place the motor where it can do the most motion. When it comes to motorized vehicles, the motor should be as close to the wheel axle as possible, and gears and axles can help with this.

5) Leave as many holes as possible while building.

I'm the type of person who gets really irritated when someone punches holes in my argument, but when it comes to my Technic constructions, I leave as many holes in them as possible. By holes, I am not talking about empty space, but I mean through holes.

As you build, you are going to find that you will want to attach things as you go, and it helps to have spare through holes to do it. As an example, it was difficult for me to build the engine with pistons in Chapter 2, but I found that I could make a separate construction and then use the through holes that I saw were available. This also came in handy when you want to create the body of your vehicle, because all of this shape has to attach somehow.

6)  Go for realism, but if you can't, fake it.

Yes, I am going to give advice of faking it when it comes to building with LEGO Technic. I find that some creations in LEGO Technic can look incredibly realistic when completed. For example, pieces that have a lot of right angles and 53.1-degree angles really work well with the LEGO beams.

But real-life mechanical creations have curves, and imitating them can be difficult. Sometimes, you just have to put on things that look as much like the actual curve itself. When I designed the Dodge Charger, I found that I had to create more of an illusion of curves than actual curves. It was tricky, and in some cases, I was never able to pull it off 100 percent.

Still, I was able to create some curves that looked like the car I was replicating, and that was enough. If you keep making enough pieces to resemble a curve, the eye of the beholder eventually makes it one.

7)  Technic parts can get strained, minimize it as much as possible.

You may discover that when you have a LEGO creation, there are gears that won't quite mesh even though they did before. A lot of it is making certain that the creation is built solid, as loose frameworks can cause even the toughest of LEGO Technic parts to shift ever so slightly.

Also, watch out for cases in which things can get jammed. This was the case with steering, as I discovered that gears that spin too fast on the rack-and-pinion frameworks will jam up, and even the toughest of LEGO parts can break. I solved that problem with making gears that turn as slow as possible in order to prevent jamming.

8)   Take legitimate shortcuts.

Yes, I did have a section devoted to building strong, and I can't overemphasize proper structures enough, but honestly, some of the basic LEGO principles are the ones that can be easily imitated.

For example, when it comes to making steering or motorized wheels, there are several ways to do it, and I recommend finding out multiple ways and just implementing the one that you will need for the project at hand. That just makes a whole lot of sense, really. I recommend watching YouTube videos on building techniques and checking out as many LEGO Technic sets from the past and seeing what building principles you can apply from them.

9)   Don't be afraid to do a complete remodel.

There will be times when you are constructing a model and you realize that its current framework won't do. From there, you can quit, or start all over again, or figure out a way to do as little reconstruction as possible. This is why I did a few drafts of the models here before I finalized any of them. It is all part of the process.

When I find myself in that position, it can be very frustrating, and there are times where you can "push it" and you find a better solution with a lot of work. Then there are times where just working on it is just frustrating and you find out that a few hours later you are nowhere near the solution. I recommend putting it off for a little while and coming back to it, and you might see the problem with a new set of eyes.

10) Always keep building, but always be creating.

Fortunately, LEGO is in the business of putting out new sets every year, so finding new projects to build is not too difficult. Much of the projects in this book are based on sets that already exist, but you are more than just a LEGO builder, you are a LEGO creator!

That is why I recommend using the skills you will learn in LEGO building to create something that is uniquely you, which is what I attempted to do with this book. What you see in this book is me, but now it really is your turn. So get out your LEGO Technic pieces, and create a machine that you would want to see.

If you want to see more, I am hoping that there will be videos that will accompany this book. I may even add more than just what you see here. For now, I'm going to use my signoff from my YouTube channel of TheGeekChurch: This has been Mark Rollins, and I'm signing off.

# Index

© Mark Rollins 2024
M. Rollins, *The Ultimate LEGO Technic Book*, Maker Innovations Series,
https://doi.org/10.1007/979-8-8688-0793-0

GPSR Compliance
The European Union's (EU) General Product Safety Regulation (GPSR) is a set
of rules that requires consumer products to be safe and our obligations to
ensure this.

If you have any concerns about our products, you can contact us on

ProductSafety@springernature.com

In case Publisher is established outside the EU, the EU authorized
representative is:

Springer Nature Customer Service Center GmbH
Europaplatz 3
69115 Heidelberg, Germany